WRAPPED UP IN GOD

A Study of
Several Canadian Revivals and Revivalists

George A. Rawlyk

WELCH PUBLISHING COMPANY INC.
Burlington, Ontario, Canada

IN MEMORY
OF
MARY RENTON

ISBN: 1-55011-073-X

©1988 by G.A. Rawlyk

Welch Publishing Company Inc.
960 The Gateway
Burlington, Ontario
L7L 5K7 Canada

Printed in Canada

Contents

Acknowledgements

I am grateful to Professor J. Zeman, chairman of the Editorial Committee of the Baptist Heritage in Atlantic Canada Series, for permission to use some material in Chapters I and IV that I had originally published in the Baptist Heritage in Atlantic Canada Series. I am also indebted to Professor Phil Buckner, editor of *Acadiensis*,for permission to use in Chapter VI some material I had originally published in *Acadiensis* and to the editors of McGill-Queen's University Press for their permission to use a portion of Chapter I from my *Ravished by the Spirit* in this present volume. Finally, I am pleased that the editor of *Historic Kingston* has so graciously agreed to have my article, published in his journal early in 1988, reprinted as Chapter V.

This book has, I hope, benefitted from a very discerning reading provided by Dr. Ian Rennie, dean of Ontario Theological Seminary. I am, of course, alone responsible for its sins of omission and commission. This volume, it should be pointed out, took shape at Mount Allison University, Sackville, New Brunswick, during the 1987/88 academic year, when I was the incumbent of the Winthrop P. Bell Chair of Maritime Studies. Professor Larry McCann, the director of the Centre for Canadian Studies at Mount Allison, greatly facilitated my research and my writing and created a marvellous scholarly atmosphere in which I could work. Mary-Ann Lorette typed a number of drafts and was always willing to go the second mile for me.

A generous publication subvention has been provided by the dean of graduate studies and the dean of arts & science, Queen's University. For this grant I am very, very grateful. I also am very indebted to Professor George Marsden of Duke University for his kind comments about this study.

This book is dedicated to Miss Mary Renton, an unheralded Baptist home missionary who profoundly affected my life and that of many of my contemporaries who lived on the other side of the tracks, in Thorold, Ontario.

G.A. Rawlyk,
Kingston, Ontario
August, 1988.

Foreword

Interpreting religious revivals is a challenging enterprise. For academics within a society in which there still are revivals, it is a challenge to take seriously popular phenomena that use means they find vulgar to appeal to people they seldom respect. Yet many academics today profess to have particular interest in ordinary people, rather than in elites. Their historical inquiries accordingly ought to include attention to popular religion, which for many ordinary folk was a primary, often preoccupying, concern.

Once we have moved to the point of recognizing religious revivals as a significant historical subject, the next question is what to say about them. Reflection on that question provides the unifying interpretative theme in this book. The chapters in this volume are fruitful forays into the largely uncharted territories of revivalism in Canadian history, preparing the way for a more comprehensive exploration. Along the way George Rawlyk, with his usual deftness, stakes out interpretative guidelines for the later work.

Most contemporary interpreters of revivals have explained them in terms of their social and psychological functions and effects. Rawlyk recognizes the importance of such themes, but he avoids the temptation to reduce revivals to what else they do. He does not take the common academic approach of assuming that revivals are important only if they can serve some higher (or lower) purpose, such as providing people with a sense of identity, self-value, liberation, community, moral superiority, political zeal, emotional release, sexual interest, personal power or economic gain. While Rawlyk looks at such multi-faceted dimensions of revivalism, he also makes clear that the people involved regarded their religious experiences as valuable in their own right.

This taking seriously of the people on their own terms is apparent in Rawlyk's rich use of primary sources. These reveal a number of dimensions of revivalists and revivals, which sometimes were mixed blessings. Nonetheless, it is significant that Rawlyk's paradigm case for Canadian revivalism is the great Nova Scotian preacher, Henry Alline. In Alline's poetry and many hymns one can sense the power, ecstasy and depth of intense religious experience. Such experience, Alline's poetry suggests, is (as Jonathan Edwards and others of the day also put it) akin to an overwhelming sense of beauty. As with dealing with a sense of beauty, one must take the experience seriously in its own right. It would be a disservice to reduce it simply to its functions and effects.

While Rawlyk displays an essential sympathy toward his subjects, he is not uncritical of them. This is especially the case in the Epilogue, which adds an important critical dimension to what precedes. He sees the breakdown of revivalism in Canada after the late nineteenth century as part of the evangelical consensus having "disintegrated from within as evangelical Christianity lost its collective soul to North American consumerism." This hypothesis adds a sharp interpretative twist to the study and makes explicit a sense of decline since Alline.

It also leads to at least one interpretative puzzle. Why is it that Canadian evangelicalism has declined dramatically over the past century (even though it may be recovering slightly lately) while in the United States an evangelicalism that is just as much infected with North American consumerism is the most vital religious movement in the nation? Some might say that Canadians simply have better taste. (I suspect that Rawlyk himself would claim this, at least in other contexts.) But that is not the whole story. The larger story is related to the relatively greater role that revivalism has had in shaping the culture of the States. Revivalism has been present in Canada, but it seldom, if ever, has been as dominant a culture-shaping force as it has been in some parts of the United States. Arguably, the United States was in its revolutionary origins a New Light nation. In Canada, on the other hand, New Light revivalism always had to compete with more powerful and more often alien culture-shaping forces. The decline of cultural influence of evangelicalism in Canada was accordingly more precipitous, and its recovery in the late twentieth century, while appreciable, has been slower.

One sign of such recovery is a growing body of historical literature, of which the present study is an exemplary part, that uncovers this sometimes-neglected dimension of the Canadian past.

George M. Marsden
Duke University

Introduction

Religious conversions have, in the past, actually occurred; peoples' lives have apparently been profoundly and permanently changed — sometimes gradually and sometimes suddenly and traumatically. Conversions still take place and so do and so have religious revivals — spiritual awakenings often involving large numbers of men, women and children. In fact, since the 1770s, tens of thousands of Canadians have been deeply affected by the religious revivals which have frequently, like epidemics, swept through communities, sometimes through entire regions and once or twice through whole provinces. Conversions and Awakenings, it should be stressed, were key components of evangelical Protestantism. This movement had its theological roots in the creeds of the early church and the confessions of the Reformation, with special stress being placed upon the death and resurrection of Jesus Christ. It emphasized that there must be a conscious response to the grace of God, and that all who had thus experienced conversion were to be active witnesses concerning Christ. Clergy who participated were to be eagerly involved in furthering this evangelical gospel. Itinerant evangelists, who had appeared from time to time in the history of Christianity and who were increasingly called revivalists, were particularly prominent in this widespread movement.

The evangelical movement had several major pulsations and a number of minor ones from the second quarter of the eighteenth century until the twentieth. It began in what is now Germany, the United Kingdom and the American colonies, having an impact on almost all of Protestantism. This movement also affected a strong minority of Anglicans, a majority of Presbyterians, most of the Congregationalists and almost all of the Baptists, while Methodism was itself a product of the movement.

Yet, despite the frequency and intensity of some of these revivals over a two-hundred-year period in what is now Canada, and despite the remarkable number of Canadians touched directly or indirectly by them, surprisingly little has been written about the revivals by Canadian religious scholars. It is as though the revivals and the revivalists who have helped coax these often large-scale social movements into existence have been ruthlessly and unceremoniously relegated to some dark and distant corner of historical oblivion by the shapers of the Canadian historical tradition. It is understandable, perhaps, why so many secular historians have been, and are, either indifferent or hostile to the Protestant revivalist tradition and all that it represents. Looking at the Canadian past largely through a secular lens carefully ground both by a suspicion and opposition to most things religious, they see what they want to see and what seems especially relevant to them today. A significant secular bias, it may be argued, shapes their research methodology and their results as they try to trace the roots of what appears to them to be especially relevant today back into an earlier period. Working-class scholars and feminists, for example, as well as Marxists, Socialists, Liberals, Conservatives, Anglophiles, Francophiles, "ethnics," regionalists and out and out cynics drill into the past in order to try to explain some contemporary obsession or concern. Furthermore, they are encouraged to do so by granting agencies preoccupied with what the Canada Council and the SSHRCC (Social Science and Humanities Research Council of Canada) proudly refer to as "the social relevance" of financially supportable research.[1]

The secular bias of so much recent Canadian historical research and writing as well as that of the major granting agencies have, without question, turned serious scholarly interest and concern away from Canadian religious history in general and from what may be called the evangelical tradition — especially revivalism — in particular. According to one scholar, the distinctive elements of the North American evangelical tradition since the eighteenth century have been a heavy emphasis on the "intense conversion experience, fervid piety" and "Biblical literalism."[2] Each of these characteristics, it may be argued, is seen by our new secular priests as embarrassing relics from a pre-modern age. The "evangelical tradition," moreover, seems to have far too much in common with contemporary fundamentalism, especially its peculiar American TV variant, and few Canadian scholars want to be found guilty by any kind of association with such a movement, with good reason. To study the evangelical tradition and revivalism seriously, objectively and with empathy is often viewed as a closed-minded acceptance of the fundamentalist position and an irrational betrayal of all that is good, progressive and open-minded — in other words, what is perceived to be scholarly.

One can understand but not necessarily condone the secular bias of so much recent Canadian historical writing, but the question still remains, Why is it that those few scholars who regard themselves as evangelicals or at least sympathetic to the evangelical position are apparently so indifferent to the evangelical historical tradition, and especially revivalism? Are they merely indifferent to the past because they feel almost intuitively that it has nothing of value to contribute to the present? Or are they, for some reason, suspicious of the past, fearing that it might, in fact, embarrass them? Or is it that they, for some reason or other, have little real historical sense and therefore lack the necessary scholarly skills to scrape into the deep recesses of past events and personalities? Or is it that their simple providential approach to history — what some of their critics unfairly call the "Showers of Blessing Approach" — really makes serious historical writing basically redundant? There may be other reasons as well — a conviction that "conservative" biblical scholarship is far more important in protecting the pristine evangelical faith than is historical writing about what to many is an irrelevant evangelical historical tradition. Moreover, according to at least one influential Canadian evangelical, H. H. Budd, the president of Briercrest Bible College, true evangelicals in Canada are — as he once cogently put it — "much busier in making history than in writing it."[3] In other words, they want to devote their time and their energy in bringing about conversions rather than in researching, for example, some obscure and largely forgotten eighteenth- or nineteenth-century evangelist or religious revival.

What seems quite evident within the Canadian context, therefore, is that the evangelical community has, for a variety of reasons, surprisingly little real historical interest. It is as though the past does not exist for many of these people, who remain preoccupied instead with the present and the future — especially the future. They are apparently not afraid to close their eyes to lessons to be learned, especially from past mistakes, but also from past successes. Moreover, as they slide into the future, they evidently see no need to locate themselves within changing society by glancing backwards at certain firm Canadian historical co-ordinates. Also, despite the fact that their actual influence within Canadian Protestantism has increased in recent years, they nevertheless like to give the impression that they remain a besieged minority desperately fighting merely to survive.[4] This preoccupation with survival has meant, among other things, and the point needs to be emphasized, that they have discouraged the writing of the venturesome and the probing studies. It may be argued that the rigid mind set established by the compulsion to protect a religious identity within what is regarded as a hostile secular environment has, for evangelicals, significantly narrowed the spectrum of theological debate and directed it away from the Canadian historical matrix towards otherworldly concerns. On those few occasions when Canadian evangelicals — and particularly Canadian fundamentalists — glance back to the immediate historical past, they are interested not in Canadian events and personages but in American ones.

There is, and this point needs to be emphasized, a great need in Canada for evangelical scholars to realize not only how important their historical tradition actually is but also how important it is for them to make all Canadians aware of this richly textured heritage. This is particularly the case in the area of Canadian revivalism — a scholarly field which is certainly "white unto harvest." Whatever is written would be groundbreaking since there is little historical work to revise. Apart from a handful of monographs, most of them authored by non-evangelicals, relatively little of importance has been published during the past fifty years about the revivalist tradition in Canada. Among the handful are S. D. Clark's seminal, yet flawed, *Church and Sect in Canada* (Toronto, 1948); M. Armstrong's *The Great Awakening in Nova Scotia 1776-1809* (Hartford, 1948); G. French's *Parsons and Politics* (Toronto, 1962); Gordon Stewart and George Rawlyk, *A People Highly Favoured of God: The Nova Scotia Yankees and the American Revolution* (Toronto, 1972); J. Bumsted's *Henry Alline 1748-1784* (Toronto, 1971); L. Stanley's *The Well-Watered Garden: The Presbyterian Church in Cape Breton 1798-1860* (Sydney, 1983); and G. A. Rawlyk's *Ravished by the Spirit: Religious Revivals, Baptists and Henry Alline* (Montreal, 1984). It is apparent that apart from Clark's book and the last chapter of *Ravished by the Spirit*, none of the other studies goes beyond 1860, and four of them virtually stop with Henry Alline's death in 1784.

Obviously, there are many good reasons why there has been so little serious historical research done about the revivalist tradition in Canada and why so much — so very much — still needs to be done. An important part of the evangelical tradition, and one that has in recent years particularly interested me, has been revivalism. In my writing about Canadian religious revivals and revivalists, as any careful analysis of my recent work will clearly show, I have been significantly influenced by three American scholars — Anthony Wallace, Victor Turner and George Marsden. Wallace and Turner are influential social anthropologists, and Marsden, without question, is one of the leading American religious historians.

This book is based upon a series of essays originally written during the 1979–1987 period. The title, *Wrapped Up in God*, was the phrase often used by Henry Alline and his followers to describe their conversion experience. The book, it should be stressed, does *not* in any way attempt to provide a general historical overview of all aspects of Canadian revivalism from the eighteenth century to the present, nor does it endeavor to examine the revivalist tradition in all of the Canadian Protestant denominations. Rather, particular emphasis is placed upon the Baptists and to a lesser extent the Methodists of the Maritime provinces, especially during the years 1776 to 1830. These essays are basically preliminary historical probes; they are impressionistic and not definitive, and they probably raise more questions than they answer.

For the past twenty-five years my own particular historical research has focused on the Maritime provinces of Canada, especially in the pre-Confederation period. And, consequently, it should not be surprising that four of the six chapters of this book should deal with pre-Confederation revivalism in Nova Scotia. Moreover, during the past decades I have been particularly interested in the Baptist experience in the Maritimes, and this, together with my own Baptist background, should help to explain the Baptist emphasis in my work. This biographical material is referred to not because of any defensiveness I may feel but because it helps to explain the essential nature of my preliminary work on Canadian revivals and revivalists.

In each of the rather different revivals I have looked at, whether they have occurred in Nova Scotia or what is now Ontario, or whether they took place in the 1770s, 1850s or 1920s, I have emphasized the crucial role played by "charismatic preachers." They are people who are widely perceived as having simple and direct answers for often complex personal and theological problems. They have their greatest impact when they direct people who are experiencing serious problems with personal and group relationships to a personal relationship to Jesus Christ — the perceived Son of God. This personal relationship with Christ, often triggered by a traumatic conversion experience, seems to solve, at least for a time, all problems arising from disintegrating and disintegrated relationships. The ecstasy of conversion, supplemented by Christian love and a sense of community provided by the revivals, creates an atmosphere for further conversions.

Despite the real trauma of conversion and of revivals, there are few manifestations of emotional excess. There were often tears and sobbing, and sometimes people would be "struck by the Spirit," but in all of the revivals I have examined, I have yet to come across one which can be characterized as being wild and frenzied. This is not to suggest that there were not any in what is now Canada. We know that there was "barking" and "babbling in tongues" and powerful physical convulsions, the so-called "jerks" and "works" in the McDonaldite revivals on Prince Edward Island in the nineteenth century.[5] There were similar occurrences in many Methodist camp meetings in what is now Ontario and Quebec in the early decades of the nineteenth century. Yet the evidence is overwhelming, when all of the revivals are taken into account from the 1770s to the 1920s, from Newfoundland to British Columbia, that they were remarkably well ordered. It was as though the Canadian obsession with "peace, order and good government" also shaped the country's revivalist tradition.

I have also emphasized the role of women and children in the revivals, especially in my attempts to understand the revivals from the inside out and from the bottom up, and in my treatment of the First and Second Awakenings in Nova Scotia I have also endeavored to explain the role of exhortation in the revivalistic culture as well as that of "hymns and spiritual songs."[6]

There are still, of course, many unanswered questions relating to Canadian revivals and revivalists. It is my hope that this study will encourage others — others which are more discerning and more sophisticated. When this is done, it will then be possible to write a definitive yet empathetic study about Canadian revivals and revivalists. I expect that such a book will be published by the end of this century — if not earlier. It is desperately needed.

Chapter I

Henry Alline: The Making of the "Whitefield of Nova Scotia"

I

Henry Alline was a man almost larger than life, and he has cast a long shadow over the religious development of the New England–Nova Scotia region until the present day. His contemporaries regarded him as Nova Scotia's George Whitefield — as a powerful instrument of the Almighty, truly charismatic and uniquely spiritual and the person responsible for the series of religious revivals which swept the colony during the American Revolution. Historians in the nineteenth and the twentieth centuries, almost to a person, have been impressed by Alline's mystical theology, his creative powers and his unusual ability to communicate to others his profound sense of Christian ecstasy. Some scholars have regarded him as the "prophet" of Nova Scotia's so-called First Great Awakening and as a "flaming evangelist" who channelled the religious enthusiasm he had helped to create in Nova Scotia during the American Revolution into "neutrality."[1] Others have seen him either as an "intellectual and literary giant"[2] who significantly affected the Canadian pietistic tradition or as a charismatic preacher who provided confused, disoriented Nova Scotians with a special sense of collective identity and a powerful "sense of mission" at a critical moment in their historical development.[3]

Alline's Nova Scotia, it should be remembered, was in the 1770s a heterogeneous colony consisting of a number of widely scattered and isolated communities, stretching from the tiny Scots centre at Pictou on the Northumberland Strait to the Acadian villages on Cape Breton Island, and then to the capital Halifax. There were also, of course, hundreds of other Acadians in the province, some of whom had avoided expulsion or else had returned from exile; and there were a number of Micmac and

1

Malecite communities as well. South of Halifax, along the Atlantic all the way to Yarmouth, were located scores of New England settlements, interrupted at Lunenburg by a large pocket of French- and German-speaking "foreign Protestants." From Yarmouth, along the rich Annapolis Valley to Truro and Chignecto, then to Maugerville on the Saint John River and the eastern outpost of Passamaquoddy on the St. Croix River, were to be found the other Yankee settlements. And on the Chignecto Isthmus there were, together with hundreds of Yankee farmers, some 750 settlers from the north of England, most of whom were Yorkshiremen who had migrated to the region early in the 1770s.

During the years of the American Revolution there were approximately 20,000 inhabitants in Nova Scotia, only sixty percent of whom were New Englanders. These "Yankees," or "Planters" as they were called, inhabited the "outsettlement world of Nova Scotia," a world radically different and distinct from the capital ethos of Halifax with its motley population of some 2,000. Alline's world, it should be stressed, was the Yankee heartland of Nova Scotia — the fishing and trading communities between Halifax and Yarmouth and the old fertile Acadian lands in the Annapolis Valley and the eastern extremity of the Bay of Fundy and along the Saint John River. This region — "Yankee Nova Scotia" — would be the source of New Light–evangelical strength not only in late eighteenth century but throughout the nineteenth and twentieth centuries. In most other areas of the region Alline and his disciples would have a very limited immediate and long-term impact.

Alline was born in Newport, Rhode Island, in 1748 and moved in 1760 with his parents to Falmouth in the Minas Basin region of Nova Scotia. Like most young people in the settlement, he was brought up in a pious and Calvinistic atmosphere. There was little in his rural upbringing in Nova Scotia that would even suggest that Alline would develop into the province's most gifted preacher and most prolific hymn-writer. He was widely known in his community — at least until his conversion — only because of his outgoing personality and his skill in "the art of tanning and currying."[4]

In the early months of 1775 the twenty-seven-year-old Alline experienced a profound spiritual and psychological crisis — a crisis that when resolved would provide the key turning point in his life. Alline's conversion — his traumatic "New Birth" — was significantly shaped by his finely developed morbid introspection, his fear of imminent death and by the considerable pressure he felt to commit himself one way or another during the early months of the American Revolutionary struggle. Alline's conversion, it should be stressed, was the central event of his life, and he felt compelled to persuade others to share in his spiritual ecstasy. One perceptive nineteenth-century observer noted that Alline was "converted in a rapture; and ever after he sought to live in a rapture; and judged of his religious condition by his enjoyments and raptures."[5]

It is noteworthy that Alline's graphic description of his conversion experience captured the attention of William James, who in his *Varieties of Religious Experience*, published originally in 1902, used it as a "classic example" of the "curing of 'sicksoul.'"[6] According to Martin Marty, James had far "more respect for mystics, mossbacks, and misfits than for the adaptive Protestant modernists."[7] Alline might have been a kind of Protestant mystic, but he certainly was neither a "mossback" nor a "misfit." Alline noted in his *Journal*:

> February 13th, 1775, when about midnight I waked out of a sleep, I was surprised by a most alarming call as with a small still voice, as it were through my whole soul; as if it spoke these words, How many days and weeks, and months and years had God been striving with you, and you have not yet accepted, but remain as far from redemption as at first; and as God has declared, that his spirit shall not always strive with man, what if he would call you no more, and this might be the last call, as it might be; what would your unhappy doom be? O how it pierced my whole soul, and caused me to tremble in my bed, and cry out for a longer time. O Lord God do not take away thy spirit! O leave me not, leave me not; give me not over to hardness of heart, and blindness of mind.[8]

For over a month Alline struggled to find peace of mind — or, as he often put it, "to be stripped of self-righteousness." Just when it seemed that he had reached the mental breaking point, he experienced what seemed to him to be the transforming power of spiritual regeneration. He described the beginning of his conversion experience in this way:

> ... O help me, help me, cried I, thou Redeemer of souls, and save me or I am gone for ever; and the last word I ever mentioned in my distress (for the change was instantaneous) was, O Lord Jesus Christ, thou canst this night, if thou pleasest, with one drop of thy blood atone for my sins, and appease the wrath of an angry God ... At that instant of time when I gave up all to him, to do with me, as he pleased, and was willing that God should reign in me and

rule over me at his pleasure: redeeming love broke into my soul with repeated scriptures with such power, that my whole soul seemed to be melted down with love; the burden of guilt and condemnation was gone, darkness was expelled, my heart humbled and filled with gratitude, and my will turned of choice after the infinite God ... Attached by the love and beauty I saw in the divine perfections, my whole soul was inexpressively ravished with the blessed Redeemer ... my whole soul seemed filled with the divine being.[9]

As far as the ecstatic Alline was concerned, the black, gloomy despair of his acute depression and morbid introspection had been miraculously removed by some remarkable divine force. "My whole soul," he proclaimed,

that was a few minutes ago groaning under mountains of death, wading through storms of sorrow, racked with distressing fears, and crying to an unknown God for help, was now filled with immortal love, soaring on the wings of faith, freed from the chains of death and darkness, and crying out my lord and my God; thou art my rock and my fortress, my shield and my high tower, my life, my joy, my present and my everlasting portion.[10]

The sudden, transforming power of spiritual regeneration, the New Birth, compelled Alline to declare — and those emotionally charged words would provide the cutting edge of his Christian message until his death in 1784 —

O the infinite condescension of God to a worm of the dust! For though my whole soul was filled with love, and ravished with a divine ecstasy beyond any doubts or fears, or thoughts of being then deceived, for I enjoyed a heaven on earth, and it seemed as if I were wrapped up in God.[11]

Over and over again in his *Journal* and published sermons and pamphlets, and in his hymns and spiritual songs, Alline referred to his having been "ravished" by the "divine ecstasy" and also to his having been "married" to his Saviour by the redeeming power of the Holy Spirit. Divine love had overwhelmed him to such an extent in 1775 that he viewed his own experience as being the pattern set for all others who too had experienced regeneration. It is not surprising, therefore, that Alline expected his followers to share the intense ecstasy of spiritual rapture — the central New Light experience — which he had so recently experienced and which he regarded as being the only satisfactory means of regeneration.[12]

Alline's traumatic conversion experience was obviously the critically important event of his life, and this point merits repetition. His description of it in his *Journal*, available and distributed in manuscript form as early as 1789 and in print in 1806, and in his *Two Mites on Some of the Most Important and Much Disputed Points of Divinity*, first published in Halifax in 1781, provided the pattern for his disciples to appropriate, to follow and to attempt to impose on their listeners.[13] Alline was eager to generalize from his particular conversion experience and to make it the universally accepted evangelical norm. His audacity[14] — some would call it "spiritual hubris" — appealed to those many Nova Scotians who were particularly confused and disoriented by the divisive forces unleashed by the American Revolution.

After his conversion Alline relentlessly attacked what he regarded as the underpinnings of predestination, stressing instead the importance of each individual's choosing freely to return to his or her "paradisical state." This could only be done by accepting the incarnation of Christ and the indwelling of the Holy Spirit:

> For that Love they now enjoy, that beauty they behold, and that glory they admire in one glimmering Ray of the perfections of God; for that Moment the Will and Choice was turned after God, they acted with God, and therefore partake of God; and thus again brought to enjoy the Tree of Life, which they had lost; and are reinstated in that Paradise that they fell out of.[15]

Since God lived in what Alline referred to as the "ONE ETERNAL NOW," surely, Alline argued, the redeemed of the Lord "must inhabit the same." For the truly converted there was no sense of "Time, and Space, and successive Periods."[16] "Salvation and Damnation," according to Alline, ·

> originate here at your own Door; for with God there never was any such Thing, as before or after, Millions of Ages, before time began, and as many more, after Time is at a Period, being the very same instant; consider neither Time past nor Time to come, but one Eternal NOW; consider that with God there is neither Succession nor Progress; but that with Him the Moment He said let us make

Man, and the Sound of the last Trumpet, is the very same instant, and your Death as much first as your Birth ... with God all things are NOW ... as the Centre of a Ring, which is as near the one side as the other.[17]

Conversion, therefore, was not only the means whereby those who had freely chosen the "Electing Love of God" were able in a spiritual sense to return to paradise, but also the God-given instrument of telescoping all time into the "Eternal Now." Regeneration was the process which destroyed artificial time and space and astonishingly transformed for each individual the mundane — what Alline described as the world of "Turnips, Cabbages and Potatoes" — into the cosmic and heavenly — the "Eternity you once, [were], and knew."[18]

Since, for Alline, each individual was "capable of consenting to Redeeming Love" and also, for him, "the great Work of the Spirit of God" was essential in transforming the individual, he felt it necessary to trace in as simple terms as possible the actual pattern of the "New Birth" process.[19] Conviction, "bringing the Sinner to a Sense of its fallen, helpless and deplorable condition," was, he had to admit, sometimes a gradual process, "altho' the Work of conversion is instantaneous." The conviction of what he referred to as actual and original sin operated with such power that the converted sinner was not only made aware intellectually of his or her being a sinner, but the real convert also felt it profoundly in his or her own soul:

> He is convinced of his lost and undone Condition in his own Conscience, without having any claim to God's Mercy or the least Favour from his Hand. He is so convinced of his helpless Condition that he finds his utter inability, either to obtain Relief for his perishing and immortal soul, or to extricate himself out of that deplorable State of Sin and Misery which he is now convinced that he has plunged himself into. He has long been trying perhaps to recommend himself to Christ by Repentance and Humility; he has been labouring with Prayers and Tears to love God & Holiness, to hate his evil Ways, and be sorry for his Sins: But the Spirit of God has now wrought so powerfully on his Heart, that he appears worse than ever. He finds his heart is hard, and his will stubborn: His Nature is at Enmity against God, and all that is good, and perhaps filled with blasphemous Thoughts against God and his Way.[20]

According to Alline, the convicted individual feels both drawn to and repelled by the Almighty. Such a person has "tried every possible way to flee from the Wrath to come and to recommend himself to Christ, or to prepare to be converted, but now all appears in vain, and he finds no way to step another step and all his Supporters are now gone." The disoriented sinner sees

> that to fly from his Guilt and Misery is impracticable: and to reform or make Satisfaction, as much impossible; and therefore like the four Lepers at the Gates of Samaria (2 Kings 7:3, 4) he is determined to try the last Remedy; for to stay where he is, is certain Death, and to return back unto his former State of Security, will be Death, and therefore, altho' he cannot see, that Christ has any Love for him, or Pity towards him; neither doth he see, whether He intends to have Mercy on him or not; yet, he is determined to cast himself at his Feet, and trust wholly to his Mercy, and Free Grace for Salvation; and cries out with the trembling Leper. *Lord if thou wilt* (Mark 1:40).[21]

At this precise moment, when the convicted individual "is willing to be redeemed out of his fallen state on the Gospel-Terms," then "the Redeeming Love enters into his soul," when Christ "the Hope of Glory takes possession of the inner Man." Instantaneously — George Whitefield, the remarkable eighteenth-century Anglo–American evangelist, had contended that "it was as easy for any adult to tell the dealings of God with their soul as to tell when they were married"[22] — the "Born-again" found "the Burden of their Sin gone, with their Affections taken off of this World, and set on things above." Moreover, "their Hearts" were "oftentime drawn out after Christ, under a feeling sense of the Worth of his Redeeming Love; at the same Time with a sense of their own Vileness, and the Vanity of all things here below, together with the worth and Sweetness of Heavenly Things, and the Amiableness of the Divine Being." Then there came "an increasing Thirst after more Liberty from Sin and Darkness, and a continued panting after the Enjoyment of God, and the Likeness to the meek and the lowly Saviour for their Hearts which before were set on Things below, are now set on Things above."[23]

Because of the mystical union with Christ, "every new born Soul is daily hungering and thirsting after its original Source, viz, spiritual and Divine Food; panting after Light and Love, from which it has been so long a miserable Deserter, and to which it is now returning." Each of "these newborn souls, being united inseparably to the Lord Jesus Christ, became Members of his Body." There was therefore a "final Perseverance of the Saints" and assurance that resulted not in antinomian excesses but in an undefined form of "sanctified" behavior.[24]

Alline contended, moreover, that his own reading of the Scriptures and his extraordinary conversion experience had convincingly showed him that Calvinism was indeed a pernicious heresy. "The lesson, why those, that are lost, are not redeemed," he declared, "is not because that God delighted in their Misery, or by any Neglect in God, God forbid." Rather, it resulted "by the Will of the Creature; which, instead of consenting to Redeeming love, rejects it, and therefore cannot possibly be redeemed." "Men and Devils that are miserable," he asserted, "are not only the Author of their own Misery, but that against the Will of God, the Nature of God, and the most endearing Expression of his Love."[25]

In a particularly evocative poem inserted in his *Anti-Traditionalist*, Alline attempted to crystallize the essence of his theological position. He realized that many of his readers would remember his poetry and hymns long after they had forgotten his sometimes opaque and disjointed theological writing:

> But let them turn, and with my Reader gaze
> Once more with wonder on the bloody Scene;
> Raised with the Cross they give the sudden Plung.
> To Rack his Frame sag on the ragged Nails,
> O how! good God, how canst thou yet survive!
> And why my Soul, why all this Rack of Woe?
> It is for me the God of nature Groans?
> How can I write? or dare forebear? I gaze!
> I'm lost! I believe, then doubt; the Scene so strange
> My faith is staggered by the stoop so great;
> And yet again I feel, and must believe;
> It must be true; its like the God I own.
> And near your Hearts, O reader waits the same,
> Knocking with his endearing Charms of Love.
> O hear, receive, and feel the sacred Truths!
> Give him thy Sins, receive his Grace then shall
> This Christ, the Conquest, and the Crown, be thine;
> And then eternal Ages speak his Worth . . .
> But O he hangs yet on the bloody Cross
> And Groans methinks, I hear but Groans for who?

For you and me, O reader, see him Dye,
And in his Death make sure eternal Life;
And from his Groans immortal Songs of Joy . . .
Listen O Heavens and hear ye Sons of Men.
"Father Forgive them" Cries the dying Lamb;
The Bleeding Victim in the pangs of Death.
Say O my reader dost thou hear the Cry?
Or canst thou stand against such melting Love?
And O he dies! but no my Saviour lives.
Ah lives for me, and lives to die no more.
Rejoice ye dying Sons of men, he lives,
And Crowned with all your sins, ye Mourners Crowd,
Ye sinking Millions to his Courts of grace;
His grace is free, and all is done for you;
Ye've seen him wade thro' all your guilt and woe
In seas of Blood thro' all this servile walk
From the [coarse] Manger to the Bloody Cross:
There won the Field in Death, then tower'd aloft
With Scars of honour to the realms of Light,
To spread for you the Gates of endless Day,
And court you to the Mansions of Delight.
O what displays of ever lasting love!
Free grace the News; free grace the lasting Song,
Free grace to Jews and to the Gentile throng;
Free grace shall be the ever lasting theme;
Jehovah's product, and Jehovah's fame;
Goodness his nature, boundless love his name.[26]

It is clear that Alline's evangelical message, in its essentials at least, reflected what Professor Stephen Marini has sensitively referred to with respect to the eighteenth century as "the distinctive elements of the Evangelical tradition."[27] Marini correctly locates Alline at the heart of this evangelical–New Light framework. But there was also, of course, an important heterodox element in the volatile mixture making up Alline's theology. And this fact should not be forgotten. Many of his contemporaries were aware of the potentially explosive nature of his highly mystical and idiosyncratic theology. In a particularly discerning critique of Alline's theology the Reverend Matthew Richey, a leading Nova Scotia Methodist of the time, pointed out that the Falmouth preacher's "tenets were a singular combination of heterogeneous materials derived from opposite sources." As far as Richey was concerned,

> there were fragments of different systems — without coherence, and
> without any mutual relation or dependence. With the strong asser-
> tion of man's freedom as a moral agent, he connected the doctrine of
> the final perseverance of the saints. He allegorized to such excess the
> plainest narratives and announcements of Scriptures, that the ob-
> vious and unsophisticated import of the words of inspiration was
> often entirely lost amidst the reveries of mysticism.[28]

Not all of Alline's followers would be as concerned as he was with
emphasizing the importance of living the "good Christian life." Even
during his last few years in Nova Scotia some of Alline's followers may
have pushed his gospel to and beyond its antinomian breaking point; but
the vast majority, it must be stressed, would be content to remain traditional Allinite "New Lights," orthodox and very spiritual, obsessed as was
their charismatic leader with the "rapture" and "ecstasy" of the "New
Birth." Not surprisingly, such men and women could sing with enthusiasm the "New Light" hymn and make it their own unique testimony:

> Come all who are New-Lights indeed,
> Who are from sin and bondage freed;
> From Egypts land we've took our flight,
> For God has given us a New-Light.

> Long time we with the wicked trod,
> And madly ran the sinful road;
> Against the gospel we did fight,
> Scar'd at the name of a New-Light.

> At length the Lord in mercy call'd,
> And gave us strength to give up all;
> He gave us grace to choose aright,
> A portion with despised New-Lights.

> Though by the world we are disdain'd,
> And have our names cast out by men;
> Yet Christ our captain for us fights,
> Nor death, nor hell, can hurt New-Lights.

> I know not any sect or part,
> But such as are New-Lights in heart;

If in Christ Jesus you delight,
I can pronounce you a New-Light.

For since in Christ we all are one,
My soul would fain let strife alone;
No prejudice can any bear,
Nor, wrath, in those who New-Lights are.

Thus guarded by the Lord we stand,
Safe in the hollow of his hand;
Nor do we scorn the New-Light's name,
The saints are all New-Lights, Amen.

Amen, Amen, so let it be,
Glory to God, this light we see;
New light from Christ to us is given,
New light will be our light in heaven.[29]

II

Not only was Alline a charismatic preacher and a controversial essayist, he was also an unusually gifted hymn-writer. He composed over 500 "hymns and spiritual songs," and these hymns contained the simplified essence of his evangelistic message. Alline used "sensuous imagery, subjectivism, and Biblical paraphrase"[30] in his hymns to communicate deep religious truths to those who sang his hymns and those who listened to them. Alline's hymns and spiritual songs articulated religious language ordinary folk could understand and could resonate with for they "represented the common denominator of plain-folk religious belief,"[31] and they superbly captured the simple essence of the Christian message. Repetition, the use of striking phrases and the creative linking of lyrics to popular folk tunes must have drilled into the inner consciousness of those who sang Alline's hymns and spiritual songs unforgettable experiences as well as profound Christian beliefs. This must have also been the case for many of those who were content merely to listen.

The core of Alline's New Light–evangelical theology is to be found in the more than 500 hymns that he wrote during the latter part of his life. On the whole these are powerful and evocative hymns,[32] and it is not surprising that for many of the inhabitants of Nova Scotia and New England during and after the Revolutionary War years they contained the essential truths of the Christian gospel in graphic language which, according to Alline, "alarmed" the heart and "stirred" it "up to action, by local objects or vocal sounds." "Although persons may sing, such subjects as they have not experienced without mockery," Alline observed, "by acknowledging their ignorance of, and groaning after the things they express; yet as I think it far more likely to stir up and engage the heart (especially souls enlightened and groaning for liberty) when they express the state, groans, and desires of their own souls." Consequently, Alline "endeavoured to be various in many subjects, to be adapted to almost every capacity, station of life, or frame of mind."[33]

Alline's 381-page *Hymns and Spiritual Songs*, his major work, first published in Boston in 1786, is divided into five sections or books dealing with, first, "Man's Fallen State," second, "Free Salvation," third, "The New Birth," fourth, "Christian Travels" and finally, "Transporting Views and Christian Triumph." Taking into account the general confused state of Nova Scotians in the late 1770s and 1780s, it is not surprising that such hymns as the following became unusually popular during and after Alline's lifetime:

> O What a heart of stone
> And Load of guilt I bear
> Seeking for help, but finding none,
> And bord'ring on despair!
>
> I mourn beneath my heavy load,
> And think I want release
> But something keeps me from my God
> And bars my soul from peace.
>
> It's hard to bear these pangs of death,
> And lug these heavy chains,
> And yet for want of acting faith
> My burden still remains.[34]

But "guilt" and "despair," for Alline, were removed once and for all by Jesus Christ's sacrifice:

> And dids't thou die for me
> O thou blest Lamb of God?
> And hast thou brought me home to thee;
> By thy own precious blood?
>
> How coulds't thou stoop so low?
> O what amazing grace!

He saves me from eternal wo,
And gives me heav'nly peace.[35]

"Peace" was provided by the "New Birth," and, as might have been expected, some of Alline's most moving hymns dealt with what he called "the New Birth and the knowledge and joys of that glorious work":

Dark and distressing was the day,
When o'er the dismal gulf I lay,
With trembling knees and stutt'ring breath
I shudder'd on the brink of death.

Destruction yawn'd on ev'ry side,
I saw no refuge where to hide,
Ten thousand foes beset me round,
No friend nor comforter I found.

I groan'd and cry'd, while torn with grief,
But none appear'd for my relief,
'Till Christ the Saviour passing by,
Look'd on me with a pitying eye.

He brought me from the gates of hell,
The wonders of his grace to tell
O may he now inspire my tongue
To make his lovely name my song.[36]

In a hymn entitled "A Miracle of Grace," Alline graphically used his own conversion experience in an attempt to appeal to others:

No mortal tongue can ever tell,
The horrors of that gloomy night,
When I hung o'er that brink of hell,
Expecting soon my wretched flight!

I felt my burden waste my life,
While guilt did ev'ry hope devour,
Trembling I stretch'd with groans and strife
For to escape the dreadful hour.

But in the midst of all my grief,
The great Messiah spoke in love;
His arm appeared for my relief,

And bid my guilt and sorrow move.

He pluck'd me from the jaws of hell,
With his almighty arm of pow'r;
And O! no mortal tongue can tell,
The change of that immortal hour!

Then I enjoy'd a sweet release,
From chains of sin and pow'rs of death,
My soul was fill'd with heav'nly peace,
My groans were turn'd to praising breath.[37]

As Alline once put it, regeneration made "Heaven on earth" not
only a possibility for the believer but a reality:

Some happy days I find below
When Jesus is with me;
Nor would I any pleasure know
O Jesus but in thee.

When I can taste immortal love,
And find my Jesus near,
My soul is blest where e'er I rove,
I neither mourn nor fear.

Let angels boast their joys above,
I taste the same below,
They drink of the Redeemer's love,
And I have Jesus too.[38]

In an especially evocative and memorable hymn entitled "The great
love of Christ display'd in his death," Alline captured what he considered
to be the core of his mystical conversion experience. Many of his followers
must have made Alline's vivid description their own unique experience
and carefully used his language to describe their own "New Birth":

As near to Calvary I pass
Me thinks I see a bloody cross,
Where a poor victim hangs;
His flesh with ragged irons tore,
His limbs all dress'd with purple gore,
Gasping in dying pangs.

Surpriz'd the spectacle to see,
I ask'd who can this victim be,
In such exquisite pain?
Why thus consign'd to woes I cry'd?
"*Tis I*, the bleeding God reply'd,
To save a world from sin."

A god for rebel mortals dies!
How can it be, my soul replies!
What! Jesus die for me!
"*Yes,* saith the suff'ring Son of God,
"I give my life, I spill my blood.
For thee, poor soul, for thee."

Lord since thy life thou'st freely giv'n,
To bring my wretched soul to heav'n.
And bless me with thy love;
Then to thy feet, O God, I'll fall,
Give thee my life, my soul, my all,
To reign with thee above.

All other lovers I'll adieu,
My dying lover I'll pursue,
And bless the slaughter'd Lamb;
My life, my strength, my voice and days,
I will devote to wisdom's ways,
And sound his bleeding fame.

And when this tott'ring life shall cease,
I'll leave these mortal climes in peace,
And soar to realms of light;
There where my heav'nly lover reigns,
I'll join to raise immortal strains,
All ravish'd with delight.[39]

In possibly the last hymn he ever composed, Alline discussed his own imminent death:

Now to the pilgrims born of God,
In Jesus's name these lines I hand,
To cheer you on your Christian road
And point you to the heav'nly land,

When I am gone and ye survive,
Make the Redeemer's name your theme,
And while these mortal climes ye rove,
The wonders of his love proclaim.

Soon I shall end this rapid race,
And tread your mortal climes no more;
But through Jehovah's boundless grace,
Saved shall I reach the Heav'nly shore . . .

I drink, I soar, I gaze, I rove,
O'er the transparent scenes of bliss,
Still lost with wonder in his love
My soul! and what a God is this!

Ten thousand blazing realms of light
Proclaim their God, and say, Amen!
My soul still soaring in her flight,
My God is all, I drop my pen.[40]

Alline's hymns are still sung in a few Baptist churches in New Brunswick and Nova Scotia. They are not likely to be found in hymn books but in the amazingly retentive memories of scores of worshippers who even today regard themselves as disciples of Henry Alline. Alline's hymns are an integral part of an oral culture which still exists in the upper reaches of the Saint John River Valley of New Brunswick and in the Yarmouth region of Nova Scotia. Few may now have any knowledge of his printed sermons or treatises or have seen his *Journal*, but they do remember some of his hymns and spiritual songs, perhaps the most lasting legacy of Alline's all too brief sojourn in what his followers frequently referred to as "this vale of tears."[41]

III

Even though Alline's *Hymns and Spiritual Songs* are extremely significant in terms of the Falmouth evangelist's legacy to North American religious life, it was his remarkable charismatic preaching which largely gave shape and substance to Nova Scotia's First Great Awakening. His two published works obviously did not. The *Two Mites on Some of the Most Important and much disputed Points of Divinity* (Halifax, 1781) and *The Anti-Traditionalist* (Halifax, 1783) were not widely read in the colony. If anything, his *Two Mites* — a somewhat convoluted and controversial anti-Calvinist work[42] — probably helped to dampen the revival fire. These two books tell us a great deal about Alline's theology, which, according to one contemporary, was a peculiar mixture of "Calvinism, Antinomianism and Enthusiasm."[43] But the *Two Mites* and *The Anti-Traditionalist* — both according to one authority full of "rhetorical and extravagant"[44] views — shed little real light on the Awakening and on Alline's charismatic powers. Alline's *Journal*, however, does. Yet the *Journal* was not published until 1806, even though a manuscript version of the published document was in circulation among Alline's followers soon after his death in February 1784. The *Journal* provides a superbly introspective and illuminating account of the spiritual travails of an unusually gifted eighteenth-century North American mystic and preacher. There is a remarkable and almost exaggerated tension between the mystical and pietistic and inward-looking Alline and the charismatic evangelist determined to preach the gospel in every corner of Nova Scotia and New England.

Despite the fact that Professor Gordon Stewart has convincingly argued that Alline's sermons and his preaching are of central and crucial importance in understanding the man and the religious movement he helped to create, there has been, since the last decade of the eighteenth century, little apparent interest in Alline's sermon literature. Professor Stewart is, of course, a notable exception since the core of his influential thesis concerning the symbiotic relationship between Alline and his Nova Scotia listeners is dependent on Alline's preaching message and how it was perceived by his contemporaries.[45]

In my own recent work on Alline, especially in *Ravished by the Spirit*, presented first in lecture format as the Hayward Lectures at Acadia University in 1983, and in my introduction to the *New Light Letters and Songs* (1983), I was remarkably silent about Alline's sermons, stressing instead the central importance of the *Journal*, Alline's *Hymns and Spiritual Songs* and his *Anti-Traditionalist*. I underplayed the significance of his preaching in these two books for one major reason. In 1982 and 1983 I was primarily interested in the impact of Alline's movement and theology on his followers in post-Revolutionary Nova Scotia, New Brunswick and New England. There seemed little need to add to my earlier assessment of Alline's impact of Revolutionary Nova Scotia. Furthermore, my examination of what remained of the Allinite legacy in the New Brunswick–Nova Scotia–New England region during the half century or so after his death unearthed limited interest in his sermons. On the other hand, his *Journal*, *Hymns and Spiritual Songs* and his *Anti-Traditionalist*, or at least parts of the latter treatise, continued to have a considerable impact on the "evangelical ethos" of the region well on into the nineteenth century.

Even though Alline's three published sermons may not throw much light on the evolving popular religious culture in the Maritimes and New England in the post-1784 period, they are, nevertheless, of critical importance in understanding Alline's relationship with Nova Scotia's First Great Awakening. They tell us a great deal about Alline the charismatic preacher and why so many Nova Scotians resonated to his New Light message and regarded him as "the Apostle of Nova Scotia."[46]

Little is known about how Alline's contemporaries actually responded either to his preaching in general or to the three sermons which he eventually published. The only available eye-witness accounts are provided by Alline himself and by Simeon Perkins, the Liverpool merchant and civic leader. A perceptive and sensitive observer of the Liverpool religious scene, Perkins, while not a New Light enthusiast, was very positive about Alline and his message. He described his sermons as "very Good,"[47] "very ingenious"[48] and his preaching as "Very Good"[49] and "Very Well."[50] In fact, Perkins did not write *one* negative word about Alline; the same cannot be said about Perkins' view of the Reverend Israel Cheever, Liverpool's alcoholic Congregational minister! On November 19, 1783, when Alline's "Sermon . . . To . . . Young Men" was preached, Perkins noted in his journal:

> Mr. Allen Preaches to the young People. When I came out of the meeting House, I discovered a Smack to rise from the Prize Brigantine . . . Mr. Allen comes to See me & Lodges with me.[51]

Two days later, on November 21, Alline preached his Thanksgiving sermon to a huge congregation. Perkins' journal reads:

> Thursday, Nov. 21st — Wind Eastward. Thanksgiving day. Mr. Allan Preaches from Psalms, a very Good Discourse. Capt. Howard with his Officers and most of his men Attend. Proves Something wet, but the Soldiers work on the Barrack Chimneys.[52]

In the *Journal* account Alline said nothing specific about the November 19 and 21 Liverpool sermons. Instead, he recorded an evocative description of what he called "the glorious work of God":

Almost all the town assembled together, and some that were lively christians prayed and exhorted, and God was there with a truth. I preached every day, and sometimes twice a day; and the houses where I went were crowded almost all the time. Many were brought out of darkness and rejoiced, and exhorted in public. And O how affecting it was to see some young people not only exhort their companions, but also take their parents by the hand, and entreat them for their soul's sake to rest no longer in their sins, but fly to Jesus Christ while there was hope. One young lad (who turned out to be a very bright christian) I saw, after sermon, take his father by the hand, and cry out, O father, you have been a great sinner, and now are an old man: an old sinner, with grey hairs upon your head, going right down to destruction. O turn, turn, dear father, return and fly to Jesus Christ: with many other such like expressions and entreaties, enough to melt a stony heart. The work of God continued with uncommon power through almost all the place. But the small number that did not fall in with the work were raging and scoffing, and some blaspheming.[53]

During late December 1782 and much of January and early February 1783, Alline continued to pour oil on the revival fires in the Liverpool region. In early January he had sailed to Halifax with his two Liverpool manuscripts in his possession and made arrangements with the printer Anthony Henry to have them published. Alline detested Halifax, regarding Haligonians "in general . . . almost as dark and as vile as in Sodom."[54] After spending ten days in the Nova Scotia capital, Alline was delighted to return to Liverpool. Here he found — as he characteristically expressed it — "the waters troubled, and souls stepping in." He felt inspired to declare:

O the happy days which I there enjoyed, not only in my own soul, but to see the kingdom of God *flourishing*. When I went to preach at the meeting house, at the hour appointed, the people were crowding to hear; and when the sermon was over, I was obliged to stop many hours in the broad-alley, to discourse with the people; for it seemed as if they could not go away. While I was there this last time, the christians gathered together in fellowship, by telling their experiences and getting fellowship one for another; and so joined in a body, separating themselves from the world.[55]

On Sunday, February 16, 1783, Alline preached his last sermons in

Liverpool. Perkins' response sensitively reflected the response of his community:

> Mr. Alline Preached both parts of the day & Evening. A Number of People made a Relation of their Experiences after the Meeting was concluded & Expressed Great Joy & Comfort in what god had done for them.[56]

For Perkins, Alline's revival had the same "Appearance" as New England's First Great Awakening. And it is clear that for Perkins and for most of his Nova Scotia Yankee contemporaries, Alline was carefully fitted into the Great Awakening–New Light–evangelical framework. Alline's so-called heterodox views were never mentioned by Perkins — only the "wonderful...Spirit of God moving upon the people."[57] Other Nova Scotia Yankees would make precisely the same point. For example, Amos Hilton, a leading member of the Congregational church in Yarmouth, when confronted by his anti-Alline minister, the Reverend Jonathan Scott, declared that a preacher's theology was really of secondary importance. "It was," Hilton replied to Scott's vicious critique of Alline's perceived heretical views, "no Matter of any great Consequence to him what a Man's Principles were, if he was but earnest in promoting a good Work."[58] As had been the case in New England's First Great Awakening, "the manner in which a preacher delivered his message was often more revealing of his persuasion than the particular doctrines he happened to espouse."[59] In other words, preachers were viewed as being special instruments of the Almighty not because of the defensive religious orthodoxy they articulated but because they could trigger religious revivals into existence. The words uttered by the preacher were not nearly as important as the "New Birth" produced. Moreover, as the French writer La Rochefoucauld once perceptively observed: "Enthusiasm is the most convincing orator: it is like the functioning of an infallible law of nature. The simplest man, fired with enthusiasm, is more persuasive than the most eloquent without it."

On Monday, February 17, 1783, Alline made his way to Port Medway (Fort-Midway or Port Midway or Portmetway) — a few miles to the northeast of Liverpool. He would never return to Liverpool. Perkins has nothing to say about the Fort-Midway sermon preached on February 19. All that Alline mentioned in his *Journal* was the following:

1.   O God, may I directed be,
   While here, to follow none but thee.
      Be this my theme, where'er I rove,
   To tell the world of Jesus' love.

2.   Then when this moral life shall cease,
   I shall awake in realms of peace;
      Where I with my dear God shall be;
   And give the glory, Lord, to thee.[60]

IV

Simeon Perkins provides the only available contemporary eyewitness account of how great an impact any of Alline's sermons may have had on the Liverpool region. Unfortunately for the historian, Perkins' responses are disconcertingly cryptic and brief. The same point may be made concerning more generalized contemporary reaction to Alline's preaching. At least three other Nova Scotians who were also positively affected by the revival recorded their reactions to Alline's actual preaching. From their recorded reaction it is clear that Alline must have indeed been a spellbinding preacher.

As late as 1856, for example, a ninety-three-year-old Mrs. Fox, a daughter of one of Alline's early converts — Benjamin Cleveland, the Horton hymn-writer — could still vividly remember listening as a teenager to her first Christian sermon. It was preached by Alline in 1780. The sermon, she once observed, "made a deep impression on her mind"; seventy-six years after the event she could still recall Alline's text, "John xii:35." It was observed that

> Mrs. Fox says she never heard Mr. Alline preach but it warmed her heart; and she heard him very often. She used frequently to travel several miles to hear him; and never heard him without there being something fresh and new in his discourses.[61]

All of his sermons and his everyday discourse, she stressed, were "very spiritual." Alline "would not converse about the world at all, except as urged by necessity."[62]

Another woman from the region could never erase from her consciousness her own vivid memories of Alline. In 1780 Mary Coy Bradley was only nine years old, yet from her Massachusetts vantage point in 1849 she could still hear, as if they had been preached yesterday, those remarkable sermons given by Alline to his Maugerville audience during the American Revolution. (Maugerville is located near present-day Fredericton.) Bradley noted in her *Life and Christian Experiences*:

> In the 9th year of my age [1780], Mr. Henry Allen, a New Light travelling minister came to preach. My parents took me with them twice to meeting. The first text was "And at midnight there was a cry made. Behold the Bridegroom cometh: go ye out to meet him." My attention was arrested, and for many days after I was engaged in ruminating and repeating over some parts of the sermon. The second time I heard him, the text was from Acts. second chapter, and three first verses ...
>
> My mind was most affected from what he said about cloven tongues of fire, upon which he dwelt much in the latter part of his sermon. I imagined the house was full of cloven tongues, and I looked upon the heads of the people to see if I could not see them sitting upon each of them. I felt an awful dread but it brought no light nor understanding to my mind.[63]

Mary Coy Bradley also remembered that "after the sermon and worship was over, I was astonished to see the people talking and shaking hands, as I never before had witnessed. Some looked of a cheerful, loving, and happy countenance; others were in tears, and cast down."[64]

Three years earlier, in 1777, Handley Chipman, a leading craftsman and farmer from the Cornwallis, Nova Scotia area and father of Thomas Handley, one of Alline's early converts who was ordained in 1782, first heard Alline preach. Though criticized by many of his friends and associates, Chipman felt that the young New Light was indeed an instrument of the Almighty. He pointed out to two vociferous Presbyterian critics of Alline — the Reverends Daniel Cock and David Smith — that

> since I have heard him and am acquainted with him I must acknowledge I like him very much and as we have no minister I cannot see any evil in hearing him preach, and this I am sure I never saw so many sin sick souls since I liv'd here as there now is and some near and dear to me and that caus'd I plainly see by God's blessing on Mr. Allen's preaching and God forbid I should say it is the work of the devil.[65]

Chipman in 1777, it should be pointed out, was no impressionable teenager or immature nine-year-old. He was a well-read, highly regarded leader in his community. God was obviously "blessing" Alline's preaching, and this, according to Chipman, was the ultimate spiritual test for any preacher. Throughout the remainder of his life he would never forget the way in which Alline used words as a "bare and brutal engine" against the mind — nor would many other Nova Scotians who had actually heard the Falmouth evangelist preach.[66]

V

At the core of Alline's preaching, as was the case with his theological writing and hymns, was to be found heavy emphasis on the central importance of an intense conversion experience. If Alline, the uneducated tanner-farmer from Falmouth, could experience "the infinite condescension of God" and be marvellously "ravished with divine ecstasy beyond any doubts" and be "wrapped up in God,"[67] so could any inhabitant of the colony. All they needed to do was to reach out to the Almighty, as Alline had done in the early months of 1775, and be "willing to be redeemed."[68]

Both the Bible and his own conversion experience had convincingly shown Alline that Calvinism as preached in Nova Scotia was indeed wrong. "The lesson, why those, that are lost, are not redeemed," he argued, "is not because that God delighted in their Misery, or by any Neglect in God, God forbid." Rather, it resulted "by the Will of the Creature; which, instead of consenting to Redeeming Love, rejects it, and therefore cannot possibly be redeemed." "Men and Devils," he asserted, and this would be the bedrock theological position to be found in all of his written work, "that are miserable are not only the author of their own Misery," but they also act "against the Will of God, the Nature of God, and the most endearing Expression of his Love."[69]

Influenced to an extent by English writers such as William Law, John Fletcher, Edward Yonge and John Milton, but most significantly by his own conversion, Alline was determined to attack Calvinism root and branch. One of the critical intellectual and spiritual problems he faced, right from the beginning, was how "to account for the presence of sin and evil in a universe which was supposedly the handiwork of a benevolent and almighty Creator."[70] Alline did so by emphasizing, as Law had done, that the world was not created "out of nothing." A contemporary critic of Alline's theology, Hannah Adams of Boston, perceptively described in 1785 his "Out-birth" thesis:

That the souls of all the human race are emanations, or rather parts of one Great Spirit; but that they individually originally had the powers of moral agents; that they were all present with our first parents in Eden, and were actual in the first transgression. He supposes, that our first parents in innocency were pure spirits, without material bodies; that the material world was not then made; but in some consequence of the fall man being cut off from God, that they might not sink into immediate destruction, the world was produced, and then clothed with hard bodies, and that all the human race will in their turns, by natural regeneration, be invested with such bodies, and in them enjoy a state of probation for happiness of immortal duration.[71]

For Alline, men and women, as "emanations" of the "One Great Spirit," shared the Almighty's "immortal Cloathing or Outbirth." Thus, according to Alline, not only Adam, but all mankind existed in this pristine pre-material state — "an unnumerable Throng of angellic Beings, brought forth in this glorious System." All mankind were originally spiritual beings, existing in spiritual "Vessels, floating in a limitless spiritual universe." It was "a paradisiacal System," where all creation was able "to bask in the boundless Oceans of their Father's Love and Perfections."[72]

Then sin appeared — not because of some divine decree or Adam's sin — but because men and women made in the image of God had shared fully "in the freedom of choice and of will which is part of the divine nature."[73] All mankind, and not only Adam, began

to view the Beauty and Grandeur of his outward Creature; which pleasing Thought of his own Grandeur began to draw his Attention, and cause him to fall in love with his paradisiacal Clothing; so that the Consequence in inward Creature or Power of Choice turned from the only Spring of Life into his own Clothing, and therefore his will not only turned, but began to increase that way.[74]

Thus, for Alline, as had already been pointed out, each and every human being has "actually and consciously participated in the first sin." This theory became reality at the moment of regeneration when, according to Alline, the distant cosmic past became the immediate Nova Scotia reality.

For Alline, of course, there was no spiritual basis for the doctrine of predestination. God did not predestine anyone to salvation or damnation. Nor was there any such thing as "original sin" imputed to all mankind by

Adam. Relentless in his attack on the underpinnings of predestination and determined to persuade his hearers of the efficacy of "free grace, free grace,"[75] Alline stressed the importance of each individual's choosing freely to return to his or her "paradisiacal state." This could only be done if the "spiritual and immortal . . . Mind," found "in everyone," was presented to the "Son of God," leaving behind "the fallen immortal Body in its fallen State still."[76] For, according to Alline, the "New Birth" was "that Moment" when "the Will and Choice was turned after God" and the regenerate "acted with God, and therefore partake of God; and thus again brought to enjoy the Tree of Life, which they had lost; and are reinstated in that Paradise that they fell out of."[77]

Despite his anti-Calvinism, and possibly because of it, Alline declared that there was indeed a "final Perseverance of the Saints." Of course, as long as one lived on earth, there would be, as Alline himself had painfully experienced, an often bitter struggle between the sanctified "inmost Soul" and the "fallen immortal Body." Yet because of his dualism and his emphasis on the centrality of the "ravishing of the soul by Christ," Alline found himself asserting that "that which is born of God cannot sin."[78]

Realizing the threat posed to his theological system by antinomianism, Alline carefully balanced his emphasis on "perservance" with what has been accurately referred to as a powerful "asceticism and bodily mortification worthy of the most austere monasticism."[79] In *Two Mites*, for example, and also in his sermons, he would maintain that "true redemption is raising the desires and life of the inner man out of this miserable, sinful, and bestial world, and turning it to Christ, from whence it is fallen."[80] To be a Christian was to be Christlike — radically different from "the world." In *The Anti-Traditionalist*, Alline felt compelled to stress that it was incumbent upon the truly redeemed to "Turn from all, Deny all: Leave all." He went on:

> I do not mean the outward and criminal Acts of Idolatry and Debauchery only: but any and every Thing in the Creature that in the least Degree amuses the Mind or leads the Choice from God. For even the most simple Enjoyments and Pleasures of Life will keep the Choice in Action, and therefore the Creatures amused from God, and consequently sinking deeper and deeper in its fallen and irrevocable State. Nor will you ever return to be redeemed until every Idol, Joy, Hope, or Amusement so fails you that you are wholly starved out, and there is not only a Famine, but a mighty Famine in all created Good.[81]

Carefully blended, Alline's "perseverance of the spiritually ravished saints" and his introspective asceticism produced what he once called "true zeal."[82] "Perseverance" without "asceticism," he knew all too well, would lead directly to the evils of Calvinist antinomianism which he had so vehemently denounced. "Perseverance" without "asceticism," he knew, was mere hypocrisy. Alline would carefully weave these two themes through his sermons, producing in the process the impression that not only was he a special instrument of the Almighty — Nova Scotia's John the Baptist preparing the way for the Lord — but also the articulator of the evangelicalism of George Whitefield and Jonathan Edwards. There was in Alline's message, despite his many unorthodox views, what has been called an orthodox "Whitefieldian sound."[83] In other words, Alline in the early 1780s *sounded* like a New England New Light from the 1740s. His dynamic and charismatic preaching produced many of the same results. Moreover, and this point needs to be reemphasized, the Falmouth evangelist intuitively realized that his New Light movement, without his careful nurturing, would fragment into warring antinomian and anti-antinomian factions. Despite this concern, Alline in the final analysis could do little to put a brake on the fragmentation process once it manifested itself — especially if he was miles away.

VI

Alline's sermons must be viewed in the context of his times, his theology and his own personality. During his lifetime he must have preached extemporaneously more than 1,000 sermons. He undoubtedly repeated himself in many of the sermons that he preached as he crisscrossed Nova Scotia from 1777 to 1783. Alline did not have the time to prepare sermons; he preached as the Spirit moved him. He soon learned how to affect his listeners positively. He used language they could understand — earthy, sexual, simple, evocative and often powerful. He instinctively knew how to link words together to create literary images which drilled into the human mind, first transforming doubt into agony, and then agony into intense spiritual relief. For Alline, as had been the case for Augustine centuries earlier, effective preaching was the "ministry of the tongue" whereby the preacher "succeed in putting Christ in the worshipper's ears." Sometimes his preaching, "charged with emotionalism," delivered in a "fervent and eloquent manner" in a resonating tenor voice, became superb poetry. Sometimes the poetry was sung as a spiritual song, which was then immediately followed by an almost frenzied outburst of words directed at specific people in his audience. This too was an important characteristic of Alline's preaching. He loved to direct certain themes in his sermons at certain people — at the young, at the old, at the fishermen, at the community leaders, at the soldiers. People who heard Alline must have felt that he was preaching especially *to* them and *at* them, and hundreds positively responded to this form of directed intimacy.

It is not surprising that the Reverend Jonathan Scott bitterly complained that Alline's books and sermons were "interspersed with Poetry calculated to excite and raise the Passions of the Reader, especially the young, ignorant and inconsistent, who are influenced more by the Sound and Giggle of the words, than by solid Sentences and rational and scriptural Ideas of divine and eternal Things; and hereby are prepared to take in, and embrace all the destructive and Religion-destroying and Soul-destroying Sentiments contained therein."[84] Scott's observation tells us why Alline was such a success in Nova Scotia, and Scott such a failure. Alline appealed to the "Passions," especially of the young. Scott appealed to the head — to the "rational." Alline articulated the novel, the experiential, while Scott mouthed orthodox shibboleths. Alline's preaching triggered a widespread revival; Scott's "solid" and "rational" preaching resulted in indifference and spiritual apathy. Scott seemed to point back to an increasingly irrelevant Calvinist past; Alline, on the other hand, appeared to thrust his listeners into the future — a future promising "individual liberty" and eternal hope. One of Alline's popular hymns made the point in this way:

> And Hail a Brighter Morning near
> When Heavens great Sun Shall once appear
> All Suns and Stars Shall Cease to Shine
> But this Eternal Sun of Mine.
>
> Far, Far, from interposing Night
> Awake in Uncreated Light
> My raptured Soul with all the throng
> Shall Join in Heavens immortal Song.[85]

While in southern Nova Scotia, Scott may have been a failure as a preacher and pastor. He was, however, an astute and caustic critic of Alline and his theology. In *A Brief View of the Religious Tenets, and Sentiments... of Mr. Henry Alline*, published in Halifax in the summer of 1784, Scott aimed specifically at *Two Mites, The Anti-Traditionist* and the Liverpool sermon of November 19, 1782. Scott not only presented a "faithful picture ... of Puritan orthodoxy as it was preached in Nova Scotia,"[86] but he also convincingly showed how successful Alline had been in destroying Calvinist "Tradition and Order."[87]

Scott devoted twenty pages of *A Brief View*, "Section XIII," to Alline's Liverpool sermon.[88] It is the only available contemporary critique of the sermon and, without question, the most detailed ever written. It is noteworthy that Scott concentrated on what he regarded as Alline's heretical interpretation of the Scriptures, of the atonement and of the incarnation, yet he also had to admit that Alline's view of conversion was indeed virtually the same as the orthodox New England evangelical version. "Our Author," Scott maintained, "allows of no Imputation of the Righteousness of Christ to Sinners, 'but the pure Spirit of Christ in them' in which Expressions he confounds, or rather wholly excludes Justification by Faith in the Righteousness of Christ, while he is teaching the Infusion of Grace into the Soul in Regeneration and Sanctification." Then Scott concludes:

> But we must not give up the Doctrine of Justification by the Righteousness of Christ imputed, to make Way for the Doctrine of Regeneration and Sanctification by the Holy Spirit, seeing both as taught with great Plainness, and the former as well as the latter in the Holy Scriptures; and have a perfect Consistence and Agreement with each other: And as Things are constituted, the former is as absolutely necessary and essential to our Salvation, as the latter.[89]

Alline would have probably replied that his half a loaf was infinitely better than Scott's whole loaf.

VII

Why was Alline such a successful preacher? A variety of answers have already been provided, or at least alluded to. He was successful, it has been argued, because his "New Light–evangelical" message provided answers to disoriented and confused Nova Scotians desperately looking for meaning in life. His message was widely regarded as infused by charismatic power. It was felt that he was an inspired instrument of the Almighty, not only because he said that he was but also because his preaching resulted in conversions — many of them. The reasoning might have been circuitous, yet it was also convincing to his contemporaries. There was a widespread revival in Nova Scotia, Alline was the key evangelist in the revival, and hence Alline's preaching was the means whereby the Holy Spirit swept across the colony.[90]

It should be remembered that in his preaching Alline emphasized the fact that he was in direct communication with the Almighty, who inspired his every word and every action. Not only had he experienced God directly through "the scriptures," not only had he actually heard "the still small voice" of God, but he had also, for what seemed to be an eternal moment, actually seen the Almighty. At all levels of sensory experience Alline had been overwhelmed by the divine presence, which had penetrated the deepest recesses of his being.[91] It is not surprising, therefore, that when he preached, Alline underscored the fact that he was indeed a special intermediary between God and his fellow Nova Scotians and New Englanders. "The Lord," Alline frequently informed his receptive hearers, "is come with a stammering tongue, to seek you."[92]

Christ evidently spoke to Nova Scotians by Alline's "stammering tongue." Alline's heretical views and his anti-Calvinism did little to dissuade the thousands who flocked to hear "that man of God"[93] from their conviction that Alline indeed possessed divine and supernatural sanction and power. He succeeded in juxtaposing fear and anxiety with love and security. Yet the question must be asked: Why was Alline's "free grace" gospel so readily accepted in those areas of the colony where Calvinism had hitherto been widely regarded as the orthodox norm? Did Alline, almost singlehandedly, shatter the old Calvinist hegemony over Yankee Nova Scotia? According to Maurice Armstrong, this is precisely what he did. Alline's mystical pietism helped to transform the Calvinist–Puritan obsession with order and deference into a "growing appreciation of the dignity and rights of man" and the crucial importance "of personal and political freedom."[94] Armstrong's assertion, unfortunately, is not supported by any references to the Nova Scotia situation either during or after the Awakening. Moreover, Armstrong does not try to develop his argument that Alline's revival was Nova Scotia's American Revolution and the means whereby the foundations of Calvinism were, once and for all, completely undermined.

In the short run, Alline certainly weakened Calvinism's hold on Yankee Nova Scotia, but it should never be forgotten that he refused to abandon a key theological construct of Calvinism: the perseverance of the saints. This may help to explain why people who might regard themselves as orthodox Calvinists could still accept his message. Alline's emphasis on free grace meant that at the human side of the cosmic equation there would be certainty — a certainty that could never be provided by Calvinism and predestination. In the late 1770s and early 1780s, many people in Nova Scotia were looking for a religious experience which they could themselves trigger. Alline's preaching obviously provided this. But they were also looking for Calvinist assurance. In a sense, Alline provided them with best of both worlds: they edged into a nineteenth-century Arminian future yet could look back to their Puritan Calvinist past in seventeenth-century New England.

That Alline's free grace gospel did *not*, in fact, destroy Calvinism in Nova Scotia in the long run is convincingly demonstrated by the history of the Baptist movement in the province.[95] The Baptists considered themselves in the post-1800 period to be the inheritors of Alline's New Light tradition. The Baptist majority in Nova Scotia, led by such early disciples of Alline as Thomas Handley Chipman, Edward and James Manning and Joseph Dimock, among others, moved their denomination toward Calvinist order and away from Alline's New Light free grace. There would be ardent advocates of the "free will" Allinite position within the Baptist tradition in Nova Scotia, but they would find themselves a rather insignificant minority.

On the other hand, as the nineteenth century unfolded in neighboring New Brunswick, the Allinite–Free Will component of the burgeoning Baptist movement was much larger and more influential than in Nova Scotia. In the census of 1871, for example, out of a total Nova Scotia population of 387,800 there were 54,263 "Regular" (Calvinist) Baptists, 14.7 percent of the population, and 19,032 "Free" Baptists, or 4.9 percent of the total population. In New Brunswick, on the other hand, out of a population of 285,594 there were 42,729 "Regular" Baptists, 15 percent of the population, and 27,866 "Free" Baptists, 9.8 percent of all New Brunswickers.[96] As David Bell has persuasively argued, it was ironic that Henry Alline should have had a greater long-term impact on New Brunswick — the Loyalist province, which was created in the year of his death — than in his home province of Nova Scotia.[97]

Alline's preaching convincingly shows that, as the Methodist *Book of Discipline* expressed it, "the best general method" of evangelistic preaching had to accomplish four results: "1. To convince: 2. To offer Christ: 3. To invite: 4. To build up." And this had to be done "in some measure in every sermon."[98] Alline, though not a Methodist, certainly in all of his preaching was faithful to the *Book of Discipline*. He was an extraordinarily gifted evangelist; the existing historical evidence makes this point abundantly clear. Alline, it may be argued, taking into account his immediate and long-term impact, "stands unrivalled," as David Bell has recently argued, "as the greatest 'Canadian' of the eighteenth century, the greatest Maritimer of any age and the most significant religious figure this country has yet produced."[99]

Chapter II

Henry Alline and Nova Scotia's
"First Great Awakening"

I

On experiencing his "New Birth," Henry Alline felt a great need in April 1775 to share his new-found evangelical faith with his parents. "Surrounded by the arms of everlasting love," as he explained it, and happily resting "in the arms of redeeming love," Alline rushed down to his parents at sunrise to declare to them "the miracle of God's unbounded grace to me." In this act Alline was asserting both his independence and his dependence. For the first time in his life Alline explained to his parents what the Bible actually taught about the "love and condescension of an infinite God" and then, also for the first time, he led the morning prayers, to the delight and amazement of his mother and father and siblings. "I had never been heard to speak even one word of my own standing," he observed, "nor ever known to pray either in public or private." Yet Alline was actually afraid to tell his parents about his decision "to preach, ... keeping that in my own mind." The "New Birth" was something his parents could quite happily accept — regarding it as an integral part of their Yankee Congregational heritage, but any decision on his part to challenge the traditional role of the "educated ministry" was obviously anathema to his mother and father. Looking back at his procrastination, Alline once commented:

I have since thought, it was the work of the devil, to keep it concealed, for it kept me back from public improvement, longer than perhaps otherwise I might have done, and caused me to pass many a sorrowful hour, not knowing what to do; I having no one to tell my mind to, or ask advice from, who perhaps might have been instru-

32

mental in God's hand of helping me out, and shewing me the way of duty.[1]

While he pondered his fate and tried to summon sufficient courage to cut his future from his parents' present and past, Alline found great pleasure in walking over the vast expanse of Falmouth dykeland "in private for hours and hours," where he "conversed with God oftentimes as with an intimate friend, and feasted on his love." These conversations, however, did not help Alline resolve his dilemma about what he referred to as his "call to the ministry." Throughout the period from April 1775 to May 1776, Alline could think "of little or nothing else" but preaching his unique brand of "New Light" Christianity. At first he was satisfied with merely witnessing to his close friends — people like his brother-in-law John Payzant. Gradually, "the glorious work of God began to spread in that dark land," as Alline deflected the youthful enthusiasm of his young "frolicking" friends into religious introspection and then conversion. As the revival, or the "New Light Stir," spread, Alline felt himself under increasing pressure to "come out, and attempt to speak in public." He felt that "it would have been very easy for me, believing that God would go with me"; yet Alline was also painfully aware of the "prejudices of education and the strong ties of tradition" which "so chained me down, that I could not think myself qualified for it, without having a great deal of human learning." Alline went on to point out that despite the fact that he

had not the least doubt, but God had called me to the ministry, yet I could not believe, that it was his will, that I should preach, until he had found out some way to get me qualified by human assistance, for I thought I must go, but could not go without learning, neither could I believe that God expected that I should go without it. O the strong chains of tradition, and the great prejudices of education! how many trials and heavy hours might I have escaped, if I could have believed that God would or ever could call any one to the work of the ministry, with no more human learning, than what I had.[2]

A desperate Alline, fearful that "the prime of my days would be over" before being "employed in the cause of Christ," finally summoned enough courage to talk about his problem with one of his brothers-in-law — possibly John Payzant. He wanted to be prodded into preaching; but his brother-in-law, who was also "under the chains ... respecting human learning," merely advised Alline "to apply [himself] immediately to reading and studying until some door opened to me to attain to more learning." Feeling in October 1775 that he had been directed by the Holy Spirit to "proceed to New-England ... to get learning there," Alline made his way to Cornwallis, from which centre a vessel was to sail shortly for Boston. Alline carefully avoided telling his parents why he was going to Massachusetts; according to them, he was sailing there in order to see relatives and also to flee from the aggressive British "press-gangs" — then sweeping the province in search for badly needed recruits for the British navy.[3]

It is remarkable that Alline at this crucial turning point in his life was still carefully hiding his real motivation from his parents. He was obviously intimidated by them and by the religious values which they symbolized. Here was a man, almost twenty-eight years old, traumatized only months before by an intense conversion experience, who could not tell his parents that he had to return to New England in order to be properly educated there for the Christian ministry. Did deference, intimidation and fear account for Alline's peculiar behavior — some would call it dishonesty? Why was the man who had experienced first-hand the "ecstacies of joy, praising and adoring the Ancient of Days, for his free and unbounded grace" so reluctant to explain his real religious feelings to his parents? There are no easy answers to these questions. It seems that Alline, like many children, could not express openly his deepest anxieties to his parents. There was a communication gap that he felt incapable of bridging, and, moreover, he intuitively feared that his mother and father, fully aware of his shortcomings and vulnerabilities and powerfully attached to Congregational and Calvinist traditionalism, would emphatically criticize and reject his decision to become a minister of the gospel. To avoid this anticipated rejection, Alline told them nothing about his real reasons for going to Boston. Once properly educated, he would return to Nova Scotia, with his New England "learning" assuage his parents and serve his Redeemer at the same time.

In the late autumn of 1775, Alline waited in Cornwallis for the ship to set sail for Boston, but the vessel "was seized," and its owners decided to delay the voyage until the spring of the following year. Alline could not be certain if the delay had been brought about by the Devil or by the Almighty. An outbreak of an epidemic of smallpox in the Falmouth region only served to exacerbate his anxiety and his guilt, as did mounting societal pressure directed to him to become active in the local militia.[4]

During the winter months of 1775 and 1776 Alline's views regarding education and the Christian ministry underwent a significant change, and by April 14, 1776, he at last felt that he could declare his independence of his parents and all that they represented. News about the Anglo-American conflict in the Thirteen Colonies had persuaded Alline that returning to New England to be educated there no longer made very much sense. Moreover the news triggered in Alline what the Falmouth tanner-farmer described as God's breaking "into my soul with the revivals of his grace, the sweetness of his love":

> The vanity of all things here below, and the worth of souls . . . gave me such a longing desire to go forth with the gospel, and proclaim the Redeemer's name, that my soul cried out, Send me, send me, O Lord God, in thy blessed name, and take away all honour, but the glory of the cross, and all the commissions but a commission from heaven to go forth, and enlist my fellow-mortals to fight under the banners of King Jesus: and my soul rejoices to take it for my whole portion, while on this mortal stage.[5]

Christ alone and not George III or the Patriots alone merited unquestioning allegiance, and Alline was determined to be involved, not in what he referred to as the "inhuman" civil war, but in the cosmic battle then raging between his Redeemer and the minions of the Devil. The Anglo-American crisis further helped to shape Alline's resolve "to preach the gospel," as did some strong advice from yet another of his brothers-in-law.

His brother-in-law bluntly asked Alline what he was waiting for. If God had called him, he "ought immediately to go, and not wait for any more learning." Alline limply replied, "Although I was convinced that God had called me, yet I could not think that it was his will for me to proceed, until that he had given me more human wisdom." "Why?" answered his brother-in-law. "Has not Christ learning enough?" "Is he not able to teach you in half an hour in his school, more than you'll be able to obtain in the seats of human learning all your life?" If God had called him, Alline's brother-in-law continued, then "the spirit of God's" would ensure his "success." "Man's wisdom and learning" was frothy emptiness when contrasted to true divine inspiration.[6]

Finally, on April 18, 1776, "being a day set apart for fasting and prayer," Alline met with a small group of worshippers and for the first time "came out and spoke by way of exhortation." Though he felt "some liberty," he also experienced acute anxiety, wondering whether he had made a fool of himself and had disgraced his Saviour. What made matters even worse for Alline was the realization that his preaching "was not agreeable" — as he tactfully put it to his parents. Thinking that he "was under a delusion," they angrily left the house of worship when he was speaking. "O how it would cut me sometimes," Alline confessed. "The greatest trials I met with were from my parents, who were so much against my improving." But despite their overt criticism, Alline persevered, preaching to his friends and neighbors "every Sabbath-day, . . . being sometimes in the dark and sometimes in the light; and when I was in darkness, and did not find the spirit of God with me, when speaking, I would be ready to sink, and thought I would preach no more; and when I got life and liberty again, my strength and my resolutions were renewed, and thus God dealt with me, and carried me through various scenes."

Without question, one of the most important "scenes" was the enthusiastic acceptance, on the part of Alline's parents, after much soul-searching, of his role as "preacher of the gospel." "They were as much engaged for me to preach the Gospel," he proudly declared, "as I was, and would have plucked out even their eyes for my encouragement." Alline now felt himself "lifted . . . above the fears and trials of the world." Alline had finally been able to declare his independence of his parents and they, in a fascinating reversal of roles, began to display a growing deference to and dependence on their son. Buoyed by this acceptance and driven by a conviction that he had only a limited time to spend in what he often referred to as "these mortal climes," Alline was determined to preach his gospel in every settlement in Nova Scotia.[7]

News that "Henry Alline was turned New-Light preacher" drew scores of curious visitors to Falmouth. "Some came to hear what the babbler had to say," Alline reported, "some came with the gladness of heart that God had raised up one to speak in his name; and some came to make a scoff, but it did not seem to trouble me much; for I trust God was with me and supported and enabled me to face a frowning world."[8] By early November 1776, Alline noted in the Falmouth-Horton area that "the Lord was reviving a work of grace."[9] Throughout December 1776 and the early months of 1777 Alline itinerated in the Cornwallis-Horton-Newport area — the region he knew best in the colony. When opposition to his preaching created unanticipated problems in the Cornwallis area in May, Alline decided to visit Annapolis, where he felt there was little evidence of "the power of religion."[10]

When he returned to Cornwallis, Alline confronted two Presbyterian ministers who "inquired after my right to preach." Alline replied that his "authority was from heaven," and he was immediately attacked for preaching "without a license from a society of ministers." Moreover, Alline was criticized for "breaking through all order." When the two Presbyterian ministers discovered that Alline was stubbornly "established in his sentiments and not easily moved," Alline writes, "they began to be more moderate and to advise me, making me an offer of their libraries, and what assistance they could give me, if I would leave off preaching until I was better qualified." In reply, Alline "told them the Lord knew before he called me, how unqualified I was as to human learning, and as he had called me, I trusted he would qualify me for whatever he had for me to do." "Besides," Alline continued, "the work of God was the prospering in my hands, and therefore I did not dare to desert it." There was, in particular, "a considerable stir among many of the young people" in the Newport-Falmouth-Horton area. "A great number met almost every evening," he noted, "and continued until eleven and twelve o'clock at night, praying, exhorting, singing, some of them telling what God had done for their souls, and some groaning under a load of sin."[11] They were desperately looking for answers to their perplexing personal and spiritual problems, and they eagerly listened to the simple yet profound New Light answer provided by their close friend and associate — Henry Alline.

After visiting Annapolis early in August, Alline returned to Cornwallis and then to Falmouth, which he left late in October for Newport. In November he was back in Cornwallis, and on November 20 he rode off to visit Wilmot, where he "found the Spirit of God still troubling the waters, and some souls happy" despite the "very high opposition... especially from the minister of the place, and many of his church." "O the damage that is done by unconverted ministers," Alline complained, "and legal professors." "I have found them in my travels," he went on, "more inveterate against the power of religion, than the open profane."[12] Alline was finding that, without his assistance, the revival fires were burning throughout the Annapolis Valley, and he merely added fuel to the flames. He was caught up in a complex symbiotic relationship with the Yankees of Nova Scotia.

II

In February 1778 Alline experienced his first long black night of despair and doubt. The "horror of darkness" engulfed him and "the strong bulls of Bashan beset [him] around." He movingly described the "darkness and distress" of his mind and conscience:

This was the first distress, darkness or doubt of my standing [with God] that ever I had known since my conversion: for now I gave way to the enemy (it being new to me) so that I wholly doubted my standing, that I tried to invalidate all the evidences I had since my conversion of having enjoyed the presence of God, and to throw it all away: yet I found something like an anchor of hope within the veil, which I could not get rid of; though I tried much, and prayed to God to take it away. O the unspeakable distress I was under! I could neither eat, drink nor sleep with any satisfaction; for it was wholly new to me, so that I knew not what to do, what to say, where I had been, where I now was, nor where I was going. O my soul cried out to some unknown God. Help, help, O my God: if thou art mine; if not, O my God undeceive me.

For "three days and three nights (as Jonah was)," Alline observed, he found himself "in the belly of hell." He had tumbled from the mountain peak of "ravishing ecstasy" to the "bottom of the mountains, and the earth with her bars" surrounded him. Just when he seemed to be devoid of redeeming faith, the Almighty "remembered me, and brought me again to rejoice in the wonders of his love, and to triumph over the powers of darkness." When Alline was delivered from the hell of his intense doubt, he experienced "unspeakable happiness" and was "convinced it was all in great love, yea, of unspeakable benefit to fit me for the work I had before me, which God knew, though I did not."[13]

Alline's was an amazing and honest admission of agonizing doubt; he was not afraid to scrape into the inner recesses of his faith and declare to posterity both his very real vulnerability and his obvious integrity. This basic and almost transparent honesty and openness helps to explain his tremendous appeal to his contemporaries. Many Nova Scotians, obviously, could empathize with him and resonate with the wild oscillations of his feelings.

Throughout the summer and autumn months of 1778 as he itinerated up and down the Annapolis Valley, Alline sadly noted that the religious revivals that he had helped spark into existence were often quickly followed by periods of spiritual declension and sectarian conflict. Alline found the activities of the Baptists in the Horton area particularly annoying, with their "disputes about such non-essentials, as water Baptism." When in January 1779 the Cornwallis Congregational church offered to ordain Alline, his response was to stress that he could never "be settled in any one place; for I would rather stand wholly alone in the world, than to go contrary to the gospel."[14] And, for Alline, going "contrary to the gospel" meant refusing to itinerate as the Spirit directed him. On April 6, "in a large barn" in Cornwallis, Alline was ordained specifically as an "itinerant minister." "After prayer and singing, and a sermon preached," he "received the imposition of hands by nine delegates, three chosen out of each church," from Cornwallis, Horton and Falmouth-Newport.[15]

In late April 1779 Alline sailed for the first time from Cornwallis to the Saint John River, where in the Maugerville area the "work of the blessed God increased"and Alline was able to breathe new life into a disintegrating Congregational church located there. On his return to the mouth of the river, to present-day Saint John, he was depressed with the "darkness of the place." "The greatest part of the people," he noted, seemed "as if they were to die like beasts." "I suppose," he went on, "there were upwards of 200 people there come to the years of maturity, and I saw no signs of any christian excepting one soldier."[16]

Sometime in June, Alline sailed to Annapolis, where he "found the work of God in some degree reviving: some in distress and in some sense of their danger." But he also discovered that one of his early converts was spreading malicious rumors about Alline's sexual life. The Falmouth preacher, it was asserted, had been seen "in bed with a young woman," and Alline was now "looked on ... with coldness." Eventually Alline's accuser confessed that "he had told a lie" and had "been imposed upon by the devil and his own malicious nature." Though he had never before endured such bitter calumny, Alline "learned to pay no regard to false reports" and used the occasion to trigger yet another intense revival of religion. There was much "travailing in the pangs of the new birth," and many nights he "sat up until twelve, one, two and three o'clock, labouring with distressed souls."[17]

When he returned to his home base in July, Alline discovered another kind of "distress," produced by "the enemy getting in among the christians in warm debate and sowing discord about non-essential matters," especially "water-baptism." The "vain disputes" were such that Alline resolved in August to escape by riding down to Annapolis. En route he penned the following brief poetic prayer:

Take me, send me, O thou indulgent God,
To spread the blest Redeemer's love abroad:
Send me, O God, the gospel trump to blow,
To mortals dead in sin, and doom'd to wo,
That they may know thy love, before too late
They rue in darkness their eternal state.

In the Annapolis-Granville region Alline found "the society still engaged in the cause of God: but many scoffing, making their bands strong." Seeing little evidence of the Spirit's work, Alline resolved in late August to sail once again to the Saint John River where he was certain there would be a far more positive response to his message. He rejected on October 29 a "call to stay" as minister to the Maugerville church, explaining in some detail that he had "no expectation of being called to settle over any particular church or flock." Nevertheless, he promised to visit them regularly, thus "making [them] the people of my particular care while present."[18]

On November 13, 1779, Alline was back in Annapolis, where he "enjoyed great liberty in the gospel" despite growing and often vociferous opposition. He spent December, January and February in the Cornwallis-Falmouth region, where, he noted, "the Lord seemed to be reviving his work again." After many of his sermons, some of his audience "would arise, exhort and witness for God." Exhorting became an integral part of Alline's worship service. Men and women were encouraged to witness to their faith, but they were encouraged to do more than merely witness. They were urged to personalize Alline's evangelistic message, to dissect it into meaningful segments and then bombard their friends with these verbal-powered projections — projections which, in a sense, took upon themselves an aura of divine inspiration. Alline's message was thus powerfully reinforced and through the prisms of the exhorters' enthusiasm, redirected in a myriad of directions.[19]

In early March 1780 Alline set out for Annapolis on "snow shoes," accompanied by "a young man" — probably Thomas Handley Chipman, an early convert — who carried his "saddle-bags." Alline was planning to spend six months in the Annapolis region and the Saint John River Valley. He found up the Saint John River that "the work of God was not so powerful as it had been," and around Annapolis there was stultifying and divisive "disputes about water-baptism" — bitter "disputes" which had affected the entire Annapolis Valley. On returning to Cornwallis in July, one month early, an exasperated Alline felt compelled to unburden his soul about what he conceived to be the increasingly pernicious debate "about water-baptism":

O how much advantage does the enemy get in the minds of christians by those zealous disputes about non-essentials; making that the chief subject of their discourses when the essentials or work of God is neglected. I have often observed in the short compass of my ministry, that when the christians get much of the life of religion with the love of God in their souls, those small matters were scarcely talked of, but whenever they met their discourse was about the work of God in the heart, and what God had done for their souls; inviting sinners to come to Christ, and setting forth in their conversation the important truths of the gospel; but as soon as religion grows cold, then they sit hours and hours discoursing about those things which would never be of service to body or soul, and proving the validity of their own method or form of some external matters, and condemn others, who do not think as they do. Ah, how many hours have I seen spent even among christians to prove the different methods of water-baptism either to infants or adults, either by sprinkling or immersion; when it would not at all help the poor soul in the least out of its fallen state back to God without the true baptism of the spirit of Christ, which alone can. O that all the distinction might be made only this, to wit, christians and the world: converted and unconverted. And that the christians or children of God might go hand in hand, as if there was no difference among them, since they are all agreed in the essentials: yea me thinks every thing else is too small to be mentioned among them.[20]

Alline had perceptively realized that in the white heat of revival, "non-essentials" were seldom talked about. But when the revival fires went out, then peripheral issues became central ones, small differences became matters of principle and a profound sense of Christian "oneness" was replaced by what Alline called "sectarian zeal." Alline detested sectarian bickering about non-essentials, it is clear, and he longed for the "love of the meek and lowly Jesus" to "burn up and expel" the all too pervasive "stuff and darkness" which he saw was putting a brake on the revival movement.[21]

In the late summer of 1780, Alline was delighted to spark yet another revival in Falmouth and Newport but found "not much movings of the Spirit" in Horton or Cornwallis. Alline was depressed because, despite all of his entreaties, "the fallen world is sleeping, musing, rejecting, fighting and opposing all the endearing charms, cutting, chaining, tormenting and plunging themselves down deeper and deeper into the bottomless gulf of irrevocable despair."[22] Dispirited by the indifference and apathy he found in Horton and Cornwallis, Alline, early in September, once again rode off for Annapolis, where he was soon involved in a major revival; and the "great blessings" attending his preaching followed him to the Saint John

River in October and the first three weeks of November.

On November 25, 1780, Alline was back in Cornwallis, where most of his time and energy were spent "in order to settle some matters in dispute, to heal breaches, and make up divisions." In early December he visited "the darkness and death" of Halifax for the first time "to commit a small piece of my writings to the press." The "small piece" was his *Hymns and Spiritual Songs on a Variety of Pleasing and Important Subjects* — a twenty-four-page collection of twenty-two of his recently composed "hymns and spiritual songs." The remainder of December was spent in Horton and Cornwallis, where once again Alline found himself embroiled in heated debates about what he regarded as "non-essentials." On the last day of 1780, a morbidly introspective Alline noted in his *Journal*:

> Another year is drawn to a period, and O what have I done, what advance have I made in the only thing for which I have my being? How many thousands have landed in the eternal world since this year commenced, whose die is cast and doom unalterably fixed, and I am spared? But O if I look back on the year past and review my walk, how dark and how crooked is it, and how little have I advanced my Redeemer's name and how little useful have I been to my fellowmen.[23]

Throughout the first seven months of 1781 Alline oscillated wildly between the "sweetness of that peace beyond what tongue can tell" and the "great darkness" produced by "the absence of my Lord and Master." Despite his spiritual turmoil Alline continued to preach, hoping thereby to recapture the pristine purity of his faith.[24] He was also writing his major treatise *Two Mites*, which in late March he delivered to his Halifax printer, Anthony Henry.

Alline's acute morbid introspection of 1781 was probably shaped by four important factors. First, he was writing a major theological work, and literary creativity of this kind often produces dark introspection and deep self-doubt. Second, he was feeling the early effects of tuberculosis — a disease which led to his early death three years later. It is well known that "alternating states of euphoria and depression" have always characterized those suffering from "consumption," as has what has been called a "self-driving behaviour."[25] Third, he very much wanted to be married, to have — as he once expressed it — a female friend "to lean upon." But he also felt it necessary to surrender "all up to God, let what would come."[26] This inner emotional struggle exacerbated his existing tendency towards manic-depression. Fourth, Alline for the first time in his ministry was confronted by "ruffians" and "military officers," who threatened him with physical abuse and who "with drawn swords . . . cursed and blasphemed" him. There was much "mocking and hooting" as the British soldiers from neighboring Windsor intimidated what they spitefully referred to as the famous "Yankee Neutral preacher." It is not surprising, therefore, that Alline would plaintively observe on July 6, 1781, "Yea, I found by what trials and persecutions I went through, that it was hard to have the mind in such a frame, as to suffer wholly for Christ."[27]

On July 7, perhaps in order to escape from an environment which seemed to produce in him a frightening level of morbid introspection, Alline sailed for the Chignecto Isthmus region of Nova Scotia. Here, among the Yorkshire and Cumberland Methodists and "Yankees," he was "blessed . . . with a longing desire to spend and be spent in his blessed cause."[28] Some of his former enthusiasm was returning, as was his unquestioning faith in his own redemption; there were a number of "instantaneous conversions" as women and younger people, in particular, were affected by Alline's preaching. On Sunday, August 12, Alline preached three sermons on this not untypical "Sabbath":

> God brought some souls to Christ, and many christians to rejoice in great liberty. The hearers were so numerous, that I was obliged to preach in the fields. O how my soul travailed, while speaking, when I beheld many groaning under almost insupportable burthens, and crying out for mercy. This day the church met to receive members, and according as I had advised them, no mention was made, of what think ye of Paul, Apollos, or Cephas; but what think ye of Christ. O the power of the Holy Ghost that was among the people this day. A number joined the church, and some sinners were brought to rejoice in Jesus Christ their friend.[29]

When he left the Chignecto two weeks later, Alline was delighted to be able to report, "Methinks I could say, I conversed with God as with a friend."[30]

On July 25, Alline was back at Horton after escaping, en route, from a Patriot privateer. "Let them that wish well to their souls flee from privateers as they would from the jaws of hell," he stressed, "for methinks a privateer may be called a floating hell."[31] Alline found that Christ was, once again, "all my joy":

Jesus, my Lord, I call thee mine.
I feel thy word that makes me thine
Now on me gird the gospel sword,
With the whole armour of thy word,
To spread the wonders of thy grace abroad.[32]

However, Alline was disappointed with the spiritually "dead people" who
came out to hear him, and he felt that his message seemed "to slip by them
without any more impression on them, than water upon glass."[33] What a
contrast with Cumberland. Alline looked longingly at the Yarmouth-
Liverpool corner of the colony "where I never had been." Perhaps here
there would be the much longed for "sweetness of labouring in Christ's
kingdom."[34]

III

On October 18, 1781, Alline arrived via a "small boat" at "Cape
Orsue" — present-day Yarmouth. This was his first visit to the region.
Here he faced a furious Reverend Jonathan Scott, the Congregational
minister, who "raged very high" against Alline, regarding him as a dangerous interloper. After visiting Argyle briefly, Alline made his way to Barrington, whose inhabitants he found "very dark," and then he sailed to
Liverpool, finally arriving on December 11 after being captured by an
American privateer. At Liverpool he "found a kind people, but in mid-
night darkness, and vastly given to frolicking, rioting and all manner of
levity." Soon after his arrival, a revival began. On January 1, 1782, Alline
observed:

I preached twice every day, and the houses were crowded. Many
were very much awakened; which was such a new thing (neither
known or heard of among them) that many did not know what ailed
them; but still thirsted to hear me speak in the name of Christ. Many
would hover around me after sermon, who seemed as if they longed
to speak to me and unfold their case, but dared not to open their
mouths, for it was new and strange to them and to the whole town;
for there never had been such a talk as a guilty conscience, a
burthened mind, a hard heart or a stubborn will, or about any
convictions or conversions; nor of the love of God, or declaring
what he had done for their souls.[35]

On January 7, Alline left Liverpool; the previous night he had found that his "soul was full, and the truths of God seemed to pour into [his] mind faster than [he] could deliver them." He had "everything to say to the people, that [he] desired to, and the hearers were greatly taken hold on, and it seemed they could not go away." Alline returned on foot to Chebogue, where the Reverend Scott called him "an impudent fellow." Alline replied in kind by telling Scott that "he showed what kingdom he belonged to by his rage and malice." On February 20, Alline "set out to go on foot with two men in company," making his way to Annapolis, where he arrived on March 1. One of his most trusted lieutenants, Thomas Handley Chipman, was preaching in the area, and there was much spiritual vitality being manifested. On April 25, Chipman was ordained amidst "a vast concourse of people." Alline's brother-in-law, John Payzant, now an effective New Light preacher, opened proceedings at seven in the morning. Later in the day Alline "preached a sermon, and then delivered the charge." It was, Alline declared, "almost like the day of Pentecost," with "some of the christians . . . so carried away, that they were almost past speaking."[36]

The following day, after preaching a sermon, Alline rushed off to Windsor. From there he sailed yet once again on April 29 for the Saint John River. Alline spent most of May preaching twice a day, in and around Maugerville, during which time he "had happy days and much of the spirit of God moving . . . among the people." On his way down to the mouth of the river on May 28, Alline had "an evening much to be remembered." He

preached about Elijah's translation, and I had such a sense of his flight, that I thought . . . I should almost leave the body. O the sweet and transporting attraction that my soul felt, which . . . stole in upon my heart with unspeakable joy and delight. And methinks in a degree I know and have experienced the nature and manner of his translation. Yea, never was my soul before so bore away to the realms of eternal felicity.

Early June 1782 was spent in the Chignecto region, and early July in Cumberland to the east. On July 9, Alline sailed to present-day Prince Edward Island, where he said that he found only three Christians among a "very dark people" who were "openly profane." Two weeks later Alline was back on Nova Scotia soil, this time at Pictou, on Northumberland Strait. Early in August, near Truro, Alline had yet another bitter confrontation with two Presbyterian ministers, the Reverends Cock and Smith, who called him "a strange imposter ... neither college learned, nor authorized by the presbytery." Then on August 20 Alline resolved to return to his home. Before he could, however, he "was obstructed by a sudden turn of illness," which incapacitated him for a week. On recovering, Alline found himself involved with one of the Presbyterian minsters in an especially acrimonious debate concerning original sin, predestination and the incarnation — all of which Alline had dealt with in a controversial manner in his *Two Mites*. According to Alline, in this often bitter confrontation he had clearly won the debate, and he was therefore inspired to write on September 1, 1782:

> O Jesus, give me strength divine,
> To spread this lovely name of thine,
> While mortal life remains;
> Then shall I make thy name my song,
> Amongst the blest immortal throng,
> In heav'n's exalted strains.

Two days later, Alline was back in Falmouth.[37]

On September 30 Alline rode off to Annapolis, where he "preached often and saw blessed days." Then, accompanied by T. H. Chipman, Alline travelled in the direction of Liverpool. It was decided that Chipman should sail to "the river St. John's" while Alline continued on to his original destination. After brief stops at Yarmouth, Barrington, Ragged Islands and Sable River, Alline arrived at Liverpool on November 20. "The work of God," Alline observed, "continued with uncommon power through almost all the place." There was some "raging and scoffing, and some blaspheming," and at least one critic shouted out during one of Alline's sermons, "That is damned foolishness." An aroused Alline turned on his critic, demanded silence and urged him "to remember what his doom would be, that dares to blaspheme the gospel of the Lord Jesus Christ."[38] Alline was not being interrupted or blasphemed, but Jesus Christ was.

On January 1, 1783, Alline sailed to Halifax, where he stayed for ten days; he still found that Haligonians "in general are almost as dark and as vile as in Sodom." He returned to Liverpool for a brief sojourn; there he saw "the waters troubled, and souls stepping in." Alline then spent the first two weeks of March in Halifax and then made his way overland to Falmouth. On March 26, at Windsor, he was "taken so ill, that [his] life was despaired of." During most of April, May, June and July he remained gravely ill, "and it was thought that [he] should soon quit this mortal stage." During his prolonged sickness Alline "was in divine rapture," expecting imminently to return to paradise.[39]

He slowly regained his strength, and as he recovered, he became increasingly convinced that God was calling him to New England. It is impossible to be certain about Alline's motivation for visiting New England. He felt a powerful attraction, as he put it, to "go and proclaim my Master's name, where I never had preached," especially since Alline had already "preached almost all over this country."[40] Expecting to die at any minute, the Falmouth preacher felt compelled to return to his homeland in the hope of persuading the Yankees to return to the evangelical faith of their fathers.

Moreover, Alline in the summer of 1783 knew that he was dying. He evidently wanted to die in New England, but before he died there, he first wanted "to blow ... the gospel trump." His parents encouraged him to go, expecting to meet him again only in heaven; his friends knew that nothing they said or did could dissuade Alline from doing what he was convinced was the will of God. On August 27 he sailed from Windsor, and after an unplanned stop at the mouth of the Saint John River, Alline reached northern Maine early in September. He would never return to Nova Scotia — to what he now regarded as his "native province."[41] He left behind him scores of disciples, hundreds of followers and a spiritual legacy reflected in both the oral and written tradition of the religious culture of Nova Scotia and New Brunswick.

IV

A short time before Alline's death on February 2, 1784, Hannah Adams of Boston published in her *Alphabetical Compendium of the Various Sects* a particularly discerning description of Alline and his mystical, and some would say, heretical, New Light theology. Adams' treatment was the first printed New England response to the young, dynamic preacher from "New England's Outpost." According to Adams, Alline was "a man of natural good sense, and warm imagination." He had preached in almost every corner of Nova Scotia, and "by his popular talents" Alline had "made many converts." He had also published "several treatises and sermons, in which he declares he has advanced some new things." According to Adams, the Nova Scotia tanner-farmer had maintained that Christ was never, in fact, "raised from the grave" and that no human being "ever will be." Rather, "when the original number of souls had their course on earth, they will all receive their reward or punishment in their original embodied state." Alline also stressed that fact that "baptism, the Lord's Supper and ordination" were all "matters of indifference."[42]

Alline and his followers, according to the Adams' analysis, endeavored "to support ... these ... most distinguishing tenets," by alleging "that the scriptures are not to be understood in their literal sense, but have a spiritual meaning." Alline had had "such influence over his followers that some of them pretend to remember their being in the garden of *Eden*. The moment of their conversion, they are so well assured of that, it is said some of them even calculate the age of their cattle by it."[43]

It is of some interest that Adams devoted more space and attention to Alline than to any other colonial religious leader — including the prophetess Jemima Wilkinson, the leader of the Universal Friends, and Mother Ann Lee, the Shaker "Christ." Alline's peculiar religious views had obviously struck a most responsive chord in Adams. But even though she was remarkably successful in cutting through the thick verbal underbrush of Alline's theological writing to find the core of his heterodoxy, she, unlike other contemporary observers, failed to appreciate the importance Alline and his followers placed on basic Whitefieldian New Light precepts such as the central place of the New Birth, the urgency of preaching the gospel to the unconverted and the shrewd and effective use of a distinctive pietistic language and style.

Unlike Adams, the Reverend David McClure, the Congregational minister of North Hampton, New Hampshire, who had looked after Alline on his deathbed, emphasized Alline's evangelical orthodoxy. McClure, for example, described the Nova Scotian evangelist as "a burning and shining light in Nova Scotia and elsewhere ... his christian virtues, zeal, fortitude, faith, hope, patience and resignation shone bright as the lamp of life burnt down into the socket."[44] McClure added that during the months Alline had spent in New England before being "united with seraphs and saints in their pure ardours of holy life and everlasting joy," the Nova Scotian had preached "with power to the consciences of sinners."[45] Many residents of North Hampton, though not ardent New Lights, could never escape Alline's remarkable influence. As late as 1839, for example, it was noted by the Reverend Jonathan French, one of McClure's successors, that several persons were still alive

who saw Revd Mr. Alline while at Mr. McClures. They represent every thing in his appearance and conversation as have been very spiritual and as become one just on the verge of heaven. He seemed scarcely to belong on earth. He passed the last week of his life at Mr. McClures, & preached on the Sabbath from "Zacheus come down etc." Many visited his sick and dying chamber, he had something spiritual to say to everyone. Widow Hepzibah Marston, now 95, the oldest person in the town and sister of the church, was one of his watchers the last night of his life and speaks of the prayerfulness and heavenly frame of mind with which he anticipated his departure.[46]

Fifty-five years after his death, the deeply branded image of the a-mazing Henry Alline could not be removed from the memory of an American like the ninety-five-year-old Hepzibah Marston, who had spent only a few days with him. For every Hepzibah Marston in New Hampshire, there were hundreds of Nova Scotians who, as late as the 1850s, according to one acerbic Presbyterian critic, believed that Alline "did more good by his labours than any minister that ever lived in Nova Scotia."[47] Most of those Nova Scotians, of course, had never met Alline face to face, but their positive view of the Falmouth preacher had been largely shaped by an oral culture — a culture which helped them to reconstruct an awareness of a distant past. These Nova Scotians saw Alline through the eyes of those of their neighbors who had actually seen and heard the "Whitefield of Nova Scotia," and they could only endorse with enthusiasm and conviction the last line of the inscription chiselled into Alline's New Hampshire tombstone: "He was a burning and shining light and was justly esteemed the Apostle of Nova Scotia."[48]

Despite the fact that Alline did not always preach what one Nova Scotian described in July 1784 as "*right sound doctrine*," he was nevertheless widely perceived in his lifetime and afterwards as a man "sent of God" who promoted a remarkable "Work of God."[49] Most Nova Scotians, during Alline's lifetime at least, were not overly concerned with his so-called "heretical views," realizing the centrality of the New Light "radical evangelicalism" in his Christian message. This point needs to be stressed because it is so easy to exaggerate the significance of Alline's heterodox theological views — especially from the vantage point of the 1980s. A perceptive critic of the religious life of Nova Scotia in the late eighteenth century and certainly not a New Light enthusiast, Simeon Perkins, the Liverpool merchant and civic leader, observed on Sunday, February 11, 1783:

Mr. Alline made a long Speech, Very Sensible, Advising all Sorts of People to a Religious Life, and gave many directions for their outward walk. This is a wonderful day and Evening. Never did I behold such an Appearance of the Spirit of God moving upon the people since the time of the Great Religious Stir in New England many years ago.[50]

Perkins, it is clear, carefully fitted Alline into the New England evangelical mainstream. Most other Nova Scotians of the time, the evidence suggests, would have done precisely the same thing with respect to their own religious culture.

Alline had intuitively realized that most Nova Scotians during the American Revolution were acutely troubled and disoriented and were eagerly searching for some meaning to life and for meaningful relationships. His preaching therefore provided the means whereby many disoriented and confused Nova Scotians, especially recently arrived Yankees like himself, were able to find some real meaning in the "Confusion, Trouble and Anguish" which had engulfed the colony because of the often-frenzied tensions unleashed by the American Revolution.

It is interesting that Alline, like so many other successful evangelists, made considerable use of sexual imagery in order to convey something of the rich emotional texture of conversion and the release and heightened sense of well-being which it provided. In a very real sense Alline perceived conversion as a spiritual climax, the consummation of an intense love-hate relationship which seemed to be the essence of conviction. For Alline, conversion was, as he often graphically put it, "being married to Christ," and it was a "marriage" to the "Heavenly Charmer" which would give meaning and order to all other relationships.[51]

Women and young people were particularly affected by Alline's preaching. They and other groups were almost overwhelmed by his spiritual *hubris* — his conviction that he had, in fact, seen paradise and had communicated with Christ face to face. The charismatic preacher had obviously had a unique experience; he spoke with power, eloquence and the conviction born of first-hand experience. None of this could be explained in any other terms than the ones he assiduously used to define his special authority. In all ages, confused, unsure people look for leadership and direction to those who know for certain what is best for everyone. Nova Scotians in the late eighteenth century were not exceptions to this tendency. Alline possessed, as he once explained it, "an omniscient eye" to discover "a map of the disordered world," and most Nova Scotians eagerly accepted Alline's map of their disordered world.[52]

Young men must have been attracted by Alline's sensitivity, warmth and confidence and also by the very sensuous manner in which he described his, and the ideal, conversion experience. Some may have been drawn by Alline's emphasis on the bisexual nature of God and the spiritual Christ and all those who inhabited paradise — for according to Alline they were and are at the same time both "a Male and Female."[53] Thus, in the ravishing of their souls by Christ and in the ecstasy of conversion, the young men could appropriate the ultimate in spiritual and what Alline called "corporeal" experience. The spiritual and sexual thus blended to intensify the relationship between young Nova Scotians and their Saviour, and also among themselves. For whether male or female, they could share with one another the common experience of being "ravished with the Perfections of such a God."[54] The young males could also assert a sense of their own importance in a society which had traditionally relegated them, because of their youthfulness, to positions of subservience and deference. The "New Birth" transformed them almost overnight into influential and important Nova Scotians.

Some women were drawn to Alline like moths to a lamp burning in the midst of a black summer's night. At his meetings they were encouraged to express as equals their most deeply felt feelings and attitudes. For Alline and for them, at least during the revival meetings, Christ and the Holy Spirit did not distinguish between males and females. Most of the women, in their roles as mothers, sisters or grandmothers, were apparently content to be second-class citizens; in Alline's revival and in his theology, they emphatically were not.

As Donald Mathews has persuasively argued in his important study *Religion in the Old South*, conversion and revivals provided women in particular with what he refers to as "psychological and social space." Surrendering temporarily the traditional web of cultural constraints which largely conditioned their behavior and sense of responsibility, many women sought in evangelical religion the justification for independence and collective support for what was almost universally regarded as aberrant behavior. Moreover, the "repressed sensuality of a religion which emphasized love, care and intimate relationship with Christ," Mathews has argued, "could easily mix sacred and profane desire ... into a volatile compound that provided women unaccustomed to compassionate, impassioned, even passionate men" like Alline "with an emotional experience they could not quite fathom, but which they knew excited and fulfilled them."[55] Some of Alline's female converts, it seems clear, "propelled by the fervor of their own conversions," imposed their religious values on their children and their husbands.[56] This so-called "maternal evangelism," when successful, strengthened family ties when they were being threatened by the divisive forces unleashed by the Revolution. During the years immediately after the Awakening, when they had to surrender their revival-inspired independence and freedom, many likely played central roles "in creating a narrowly maternal role and image for their sex,"[57] but they, of course, would do far more than this. Even though the revival did not produce immediate liberation or equality and often disrupted society, it did provide an important push forward as women, bonded to one another "in mutual support, personal companionship and social solidarity," slowly moved "from the abstraction of emotion to the reality of exclusively female organizations" in church, community and the province.[58]

Alline's preaching, the evidence suggests, was permeated by a preoccupation with disintegrating, disintegrated and renewed relationships. Generalizing from his conversion, Alline emphasized that every Nova Scotian could emulate him if only they reached out, in faith, to Christ. In a world where all traditional relationships were falling apart, a personal "interest in Christ," as Alline put it, created by the "New Birth," was the means whereby all these threatened relationships would be strengthened. Conversion was, therefore, perceived by Alline and his followers as the short-circuiting of a complex process — a short-circuiting which produced instant and immediate satisfaction, solace and intense relief. The Awakening was in one sense a collection of these positive individual experiences and helped to give shape and substance to a new and distinct Nova Scotia sense of identity. And it was Alline's powerfully charismatic and evangelical preaching and not his published work which significantly shaped the contours of the First Great Awakening.

During the 1778–1783 period Alline visited almost every settlement in Nova Scotia, then inhabited by approximately 20,000 persons. Lunenburg, Halifax and Pictou were the only major centres of the colony unaffected by the religious "reformation" in which he played a key role. Almost singlehandedly, as he crisscrossed the colony, Alline was able to draw many of the isolated communities together and to give them a fragile feeling of oneness. The hundreds of people involved, whether core or peripheral participants, were all sharing a common experience — a religious awakening — and Alline was providing them with spiritual answers to disconcerting and puzzling contemporary questions. For Alline — and this must have also been the case for many of his followers — the Nova Scotia revival was at its core an event of world, even cosmic, significance. While

New England and Old England were involved in what Alline regarded as an evil civil war, Nova Scotia was experiencing a remarkable work of God. As far as Alline was concerned, the revival provided convincing proof that the Nova Scotians were, as he once expressed it, "a people on whom God has set His everlasting Love" and that their colony was "as the Apple of His Eye."[59]

The implication of this conjunction of events, of civil war in neighboring New England and an unprecedented outpouring of the Holy Spirit in Nova Scotia, must have been obvious to Alline and to the thousands who flocked to hear him. The Almighty, the evidence more than suggested, was transferring New England's special mantle of evangelical Christian leadership to Nova Scotia — "New England's Outpost." With Republican and Revolutionary New England rushing madly off course, it could no longer provide the solid evangelical base from which positive Christianity could spread its enlightened influence throughout the world in preparation for the return of Christ. Moreover, as has been argued elsewhere,

> with two powerful Protestant nations furiously battling one another, the whole course of events since the Reformation seemed to be ending in a meaningless tangle. In the world view of those New Englanders fighting for the Revolutionary cause, Old England was corrupt and the Americans were engaged in a righteous and noble cause. There was therefore some meaning for hostilities.[60]

But for Alline and his followers, the Revolutionary War had no such meaning. Rather, in conjunction with the Nova Scotia revival, the war could indicate only one thing. Alline's Nova Scotia — a largely backward frontier colony of no consequence — had in fact been suddenly transformed by "the remarkable provinces of God" into *the* "Redeemer Nation."[61]

Those Nova Scotians who were converted under Alline's charismatic preaching, or by his disciples, wished to replicate all aspects of Alline's own transforming religious experience. They too wished to see paradise; they too wished to "taste but one glimmering ray" of the "Eternal Now." And they yearned for Alline's Christ to ravish them, to make them one with the Almighty. They sought the mountain peak of religious ecstasy but naively underestimated how difficult it would be for them to remain there. Many would tumble to the depths of despair soon after Alline's death, but most would never forget that magic New Light moment when they, like Henry Alline, had experienced Jesus Christ and had become part of his pristine spirituality and perfectability. They had reached out and Christ had touched them. They were certain that it could happen again — and it did, only a few years after Alline's death — as periodic revivals became a distinguishing feature of Nova Scotia's and New Brunswick's religious culture.

Chapter III

Freeborn Garrettson and Nova Scotia:
The Methodists and Baptists

I

A little more than a year after Henry Alline's death in New Hampshire on February 2, 1784, an intense religious revival swept through many of the Yankee settlements of Nova Scotia. It was a revival which owed a great deal to an extraordinarily able Methodist preacher from Maryland, Freeborn Garrettson. Moreover, it was a revival which energized a largely moribund New Light–evangelical movement by, among other things, providing it with a coterie of new, young, energetic and remarkably gifted leaders — the most outstanding of whom were Edward Manning, Joseph Dimock, Harris Harding and Theodore Seth Harding. The revival not only left in its wake a post-Alline leadership elite, but it also, almost as an afterthought, significantly exacerbated the tensions existing between the Whitefieldian orthodox elements of the New Light evangelicals and Alline's mystical heterodoxy. The Garrettson revival apparently played a key role in polarizing Alline's followers in Nova Scotia into a small anarchic antinomian sect at one extreme, and what eventually evolved into an evangelical Baptist Calvinist church at the other. The former, placing heavy emphasis on the eternal permanence of the New Birth, almost seemed eager to divorce their morality from their perceived spirituality. In other words, because of their conviction that they were indeed once and for all regenerated, they felt that they could commit any sin.[1] On the other hand, the Calvinist Baptists attempted to balance evangelical religion of the heart with reason and order. It was ironic that a staunch Arminian Methodist from the United States would be involved in the transformation of Alline's "Free Will" anti-Calvinist Nova Scotia "ecumenical movement" into what was destined to become, among other things, a "closed" Baptist Calvinist Church.[2]

II

Freeborn Garrettson, who would trigger a significant revival, and his American Methodist associate, the frail James Oliver Cromwell, sailed from New York in the middle of February 1785, and after a particularly stormy passage they finally arrived in Halifax. The two young American Methodist itinerants had been "set apart for Nova Scotia" by the leaders of the American Methodist Episcopal Church, who had been under considerable pressure from John Wesley and William Black, the Nova Scotia Methodist leader, to provide missionary assistance at a critical time in the colony's history.[3] The death of Alline had created a religious vacuum in what is now Nova Scotia, and the sudden arrival of approximately 20,000 Loyalists,[4] some of whom were Methodists, provided both a new mission field and the means whereby Black, in particular, hoped the Yankee–New Light hegemony over much of the colony could finally be broken. What Black had failed to accomplish in his face-to-face confrontation with Alline in the late 1770s and early 1780s, he hoped visiting American itinerants might succeed at in his beloved Nova Scotia.

It should be kept in mind that during the years immediately following the end of the American War of Independence, many in Nova Scotia were experiencing yet another profound, and for some disconcerting, collective sense of acute disorientation and confusion. As was the case in neighboring northern New England, hundreds of "common people were cut loose from all sorts of traditional bonds and found themselves freer, more independent, more unconstrained than ever before in their history."[5] The coming of some 20,000 Loyalists to peninsular Nova Scotia at the end of the Revolution accelerated a process of social disintegration already underway in some regions of the colony. The Loyalists, according to Edward Manning, the influential Baptist "patriarch," had a "bad and- ...dreadful" effect on the colony since they "corrupted" societal values and made many Nova Scotians "adepts in wickedness."[6] Thus, as Professor Gordon Wood has argued, "traditional structures of authority crumbled under the momentum of the Revolution, and common people increasingly discovered that they no longer had to accept the old distinctions" that had driven them into a widely perceived subservient and vulnerable status.[7] And, as might have been expected, sometime "bizarre but emotionally satisfying ways of relating to God and others" became increasingly widespread phenomena as many Nova Scotians sought a renewed sense of "community-belonging" in order to neutralize the powerful forces of alienation then sweeping the colony.

It was a period when, it had been perceptively observed, "everything was believable" and almost "everything could be doubted."[8] "Radical enthusiasts and visionaries," regarding themselves as the disciples of Henry Alline and as propagators of his tradition, became the "advanced guard" of the renewed "popular evangelical movement with which they shared a common hostility to orthodox authority."[9] By 1790 these New Lights, as they were spitefully referred to by their enemies, were a people in a delicate state of spiritual tension, "poised like a steel spring by the contradicting forces pulling within it." There was a mystical quality permeating their belief system, but there was also a secular one. There was a democratic bias, but also an authoritarian one — together with an individualism as well as a tendency towards communitarianism. For some, it seems clear, the seemingly contradictory forces within the New Light mind would soon neutralize one another, producing apathy, indifference and disenchantment. For others, not an insignificant number, the dynamic tension would result in a renewed pietism which would become a crucial link in the chain connecting Henry Alline's First Great Awakening with Nova Scotia's Second Awakening in which New Lights and Methodists were particularly active. But for an influential minority, known as the "New Dispensationalists" by friends and enemies alike, the state of spiritual tension brought about by the coming of the Loyalists, the Garrettsonian revival, the continuing influence of Alline's legacy and growing American sectarian influences provided a heaven-sent opportunity to stretch Alline's gospel to and beyond the antinomian breaking point, especially in the early 1790s.[10]

Soon after landing in Halifax, Garrettson elbowed William Black aside and became the most influential Methodist leader in Nova Scotia. Garrettson was regarded, with some justification, as a "man of varied resources, a powerful preacher and capable organizer, of genuine piety and holiness of life, who left an abiding impression on the whole life of the province."[11] His influence in Nova Scotia, according to J. M. Buckley, author of *A History of Methodism in the United States*, "was almost equal to that of Wesley in Europe and Asbury in the United States."[12] "It may be fairly questioned," claimed his biographer, Nathan Bangs, "whether any one minister in the Methodist Episcopal Church, or indeed in any other Church, has been instrumental in the awakening and conversion of more sinners than Garrettson."[13] Garrettson was, without question, an unusually gifted minister; he was a powerful, some would say charismatic, preacher; he was, moreover, an indefatigable itinerant, a man almost obsessed with — as he once cogently expressed it — "rising higher and higher in the divine image."[14] Though he spent only twenty-six months in Nova Scotia, Garrettson, it has been persuasively argued, "left an abiding impression on the whole life of the province."[15] Next to Henry Alline, the evidence suggests, the Maryland Methodist was the most able and influential preacher in eighteenth-century Nova Scotia.

Garrettson was born on August 15, 1752, in Harford County, Maryland, near the mouth of the Susquehanna River.[16] His father, an active Anglican, was a wealthy slaveholder, and he was also opposed to Methodism, considering it be a pernicious manifestation of sectarian enthusiasm. Though eager to please his father, Garrettson fell under the influence of various itinerant Methodist preachers soon after his twentieth birthday. In 1775, at approximately the same time that Alline was being converted in Nova Scotia, Garrettson experienced his own traumatic New Birth. And like Alline, Garrettson wanted everyone to emulate his intense conversion experience. After listening to a Methodist itinerant, and under intense conviction, Garrettson, who was in the prime of life, became "for the first time, reconciled to the justice of God." According to the young Marylander,

> the enmity of my heart was slain, and the plan of salvation was open to me. I saw a beauty in the perfections of the Deity, and felt that power of faith and love that I had been a stranger to. My soul was exceeding happy that I seemed as if I wanted to take wings and fly to heaven.[17]

Garrettson became a Methodist circuit preacher in 1776 and only his death on July 26, 1827, brought about an end to what had been called the glorious "story of his long, heroic, and successful services in the itinerant ranks."[18]

It is noteworthy that soon after his conversion Garrettson felt compelled to free his slaves since he now regarded the institution of slavery as being the antithesis to evangelical Christianity. Beginning his Methodist ministerial work in 1776 as a preacher-on-trial, he itinerated widely for the next few years in Maryland and neighboring states. As a pacifist, he wanted to have nothing to do with the American Revolution, declaring that "it was contrary to my mind, and grievous to my conscience, to have any hand in shedding human blood."[19] He consequently pursued a policy of explicit neutrality, despite much persecution from the Patriots. Garrettson was formally ordained a Methodist minister at the Baltimore conference of December 1784. It was at this conference that the Methodist Episcopal Church of the United States formally came into being, and it was also at this conference that Garrettson was instructed to make his way to Nova Scotia — the British colony which had remained steadfastly loyal to the British cause during the American Revolution.

Garrettson was a man of amazing energy. This, together with his remarkable missionary zeal, helps to explain the impact he had on Nova Scotia in the 1780s. For more than fifty years he preached his evangelical Methodist gospel from North Carolina to Nova Scotia, being responsible for thousands of conversions — over 20,000 some have claimed. He was an indefatigable itinerant and a powerful preacher who was, throughout his long career, committed to centralized church control at the expense of congregational independence. Garrettson once described to Bishop Francis Asbury — his American superior — a "typical" week spent in Halifax:

Sunday eight o'clock preach in our little chapel, which will hold about four hundred persons; ten o'clock preach in the poor house, where there are about a hundred people; . . . at twelve o'clock in the preaching house; four o'clock in a private house by the dockyard; and by candlelight in the chapel. I preach every night in the week. Friday visit the prisoners.[20]

Garrettson did not mention his frequent house visits, the time spent in keeping up his correspondence with fellow Methodists in Nova Scotia, New Brunswick, Great Britain and the United States, his "diligence and zeal" in studying the Scriptures and his exemplary "prayerfulness and watchfulness." He was, according to his biographer, the antithesis of "the slothful servant."[21]

During his brief twenty-six-month sojourn in Nova Scotia Garrettson visited every settlement except Pictou. A year before his death Garrettson described his Nova Scotia experience in the following manner:

I began to visit the towns, and to traverse the mountains and valleys, frequently on foot, with my knapsack at my back, up and down the Indian paths in the wilderness, when it was not expedient to take a horse; and I had often to wade through the mud and water of morasses, and frequently to satisfy my hunger from my knapsack, to quench my thirst from a brook, and rest my weary limbs on the

leaves of trees. This was indeed going forth weeping; but thanks be
to God, he compensated me for all my toil, for many precious souls
were awakened and converted.[22]

Garrettson took full advantage of the earlier assiduous missionary
labor of William Black and also that of Henry Alline and his itinerating
disciples, men like John Payzant, Joseph Bailey, Thomas Handley Chipman and Ebenezer Hobbs, a teenage New Light exhorter. But the Methodist itinerant did more than this. He not only cultivated the Yankee New
Light heartland stretching from Falmouth, down the Annapolis Valley to
Granville, to Yarmouth, then up the southern shore to Argyle, Liverpool
and Chester, but he also broke important new missionary ground in the
Loyalist centre of Shelburne.

Garrettson, like Alline, had a powerful voice, but unlike the Falmouth evangelist, Garrettson's voice was "harsh and high-pitched."[23]
Apparently Garrettson's strong voice could be easily projected a distance
of "a quarter of a mile."[24] His preaching "focused on Christ, Heaven and
Hell,"[25] but always from an Arminian perspective. Because of his genteel
background Garrettson was remarkably successful in aiming his message
not only at the so-called "middling and lower sorts," but also at society's
leaders. However, it should not be assumed that Garrettson's "genteel
background" meant that he was suspicious of emotionalism. Nothing
could have been further from the truth. Generalizing from his own very
emotional conversion experience, Garrettson declared, "To suppose a
work of grace without the excitement of human passions, is as great an
absurdity as it would be to expect a man to breathe without any movements of the lungs."[26]

It is not surprising, therefore, that Garrettson touched a responsive
chord in the same New Light areas of Nova Scotia where Alline had
experienced his most noteworthy successes. In so many respects, Freeborn
Garrettson was much like Henry Alline.

Despite the opposition of some of the more extreme "Allinites," to
whom Garrettson referred "as deluded a people as I ever saw,"[27] the
Methodist preacher attracted large, attentive audiences in Nova Scotia in
the spring of 1785. At Horton, on Sunday, May 22, over 100 people turned
out to hear him: "The General Cry was after preaching — if this is
Methodist Doctrine, it is truth."[28] Later that same day, in the New Light
centre of Cornwallis, there was "a Considerable moving on ye hearts of ye
people," according to Garrettson. And on the following day, after a
particularly emotional meeting, there was a universal cry: "If this is

Methodist doctrine, I will be a Methodist." Scores of Yankees, some of whom had first been awakened by Whitefield, others by Alline, "after meeting... continued some time hanging around each other, inquiring what they should do to be saved." Garrettson hoped that the revival would give the radical Allinites (those followers of Alline who were pushing his gospel toward antinomianism) a fatal and what the Methodist preacher termed a "wonderful Stab."[29]

Preaching at a minimum three sermons each Sunday, in barns, private homes and Baptist and Presbyterian churches, and once each day of the week, Garrettson continued to itinerate up and down the Annapolis Valley from Windsor to Annapolis throughout June and July, 1785. In late July he visited Liverpool and a month later made his way to the Loyalist centre of Shelburne. Garrettson noted in his journal:

> Our dear Master began to carry on a blessed work; but the devil and his children were angry. They frequently stoned the house; and one night a company came out, and strove (as it stood by the brow of a hill on pillars) to shove it down — whilst I was preaching to near four hundred people by candlelight, they were beating underneath, to get away the pillars. In the midst of my preaching I cried out, *Without are dogs, sorcerers, whore mongers, idolaters, and whoever loveth and maketh a lie.* The company ran off with a hideous yelling, and we were left to worship God peaceably.

Then Garrettson went on: "During my stay in and around Shelburne (which was six weeks) numbers both white and black, were added to the society; and many tested the good word of God, and felt the powers of the world to come."[30]

In the early autumn of 1785 Garrettson returned to Halifax; he took charge of the extensive Halifax circuit, which included regular visits to Windsor, Cornwallis and Horton. In the spring of 1786 Garrettson once again visited Liverpool, where he observed to John Wesley that though "Alline's small party oppose us warmly, the greater part of the town attend our ministry, and the first people have joined our society."[31] After this success Garrettson made his way to the Loyalist centre Shelburne, now a town in serious decline, and on to Barrington. At first the people of Barrington were unresponsive, having been warned by Thomas Handley Chipman, the New Light and Baptist minister located at Granville, that Garrettson was "a dangerous 'Arminian.'" Despite Chipman's warning, however, hundreds turned out to listen to the visiting Methodist from

Maryland. "Between two and three hundred were awakened in a greater or less degree," reported a delighted Garrettson, and "their shyness and prejudices were all removed."[32]

Scores of people in settlements along the South Shore, in places like Barrington and Cape Negro, were converted, Garrettson was certain, and because of what he called "this visitation of the Spirit," Methodist churches were organized on what was then called the "Arminian plan."[33] The stress placed on "free grace," the possibility of the "second blessing" — the Methodist experience of sanctification — and the warm fellowship of the "class meeting" all appealed to those Nova Scotians who wanted Alline's evangelical Christianity but not the excesses of some of his follow- ers. Garrettson described an especially memorable Sunday during his Barrington sojourn in the following manner:

> This morning my mind was amazingly distressed. I was afraid the Lord had not called me to this town. I mourned in secret, and entreated the Lord to make it manifest that he had sent me to his place, by a display of his convincing power among the people. The hour came, and I repaired to the meeting-house; none were present but my pilot (and he was greatly shaken, and in doubt which way to go) and two others. My distress of mind was to be sensibly felt. I withdrew to a little wood, a quarter of a mile from the meeting- house, and entreated the Lord, if he required me to preach in the place, to send out the people and bless his word. As I was again ascending the hill toward the meeting-house, resolving within my- self: that if the people did not attend, and if the word was not blest, I would leave the town, and conclude that I was not called thereto. But I saw the people coming from every part of the town, and in a short time, we had a large gathering, and immediately the cloud broke from my mind, and with a glad heart I ascended the pulpit stairs; and the word of the Lord seemed all open to me. I preached, and the flame ran through the assembly: in the afternoon I preached again, with the same freedom. Among two or three hundred people it appeared as though there were but few present, but in a greater or less degree felt the flame. After meeting was ended, they came around me on every hand in tears; and I suppose I had invitations to more than twenty houses.[34]

In the autumn of 1786 Garrettson returned to Halifax, and in the winter months of 1786 and 1787 he was largely responsible for coaxing into existence yet another revival in Horton and Cornwallis. "I have had a blessed winter among them," Garrettson observed to John Wesley on March 10, 1787. "If the work continues much longer as it has done, the greater part of the people will be brought in." In Horton especially, there had "been a divine display; many convinced and converted to God." Garrettson also noted:

> God is carrying on his work in a glorious manner in Barrington; the people flock from every quarter to hear the word: many have been convinced, and about fourteen have been set at liberty, some of whom were famous for all manner of wickedness. The fields here seem white for harvest.[35]

Despite the Nova Scotia "white fields" all "ready for harvest," Garrettson left the colony one month later for the United States, having "received a letter from Dr. Coke [who would succeed Wesley] in which [he] was requested to attend the Baltimore Conference." "It was with reluctance I came to this country," he observed at the time, "but I now feel a willingness to labour and suffer in the cause of God, among this people."[36] Garrettson, however, would never return — not only because of his strong sense of being and wanting to remain an American, especially once he had returned to his homeland, but also because, as he once cogently put it, "I was not clear that I had a call to leave the United States."[37]

Nova Scotia Methodism would suffer greatly because of this decision. When Garrettson left the colony, there were almost 600 Methodist Church members out of a total population of approximately 30,000. There were probably seven or eight times as many adherents and supporters as there were official members. The Methodists had not only made inroads in the Yankee settlements, but they had also been particularly successful among the Yorkshire immigrants and among the Black Loyalists. There were, in fact, ten times as many Methodist Church members as there were Baptists, and probably three times as many as there were actual New Light Congregationalists in their two organized churches, Chipman's at Granville and the Reverend John Payzant's at Horton and Cornwallis. Indeed, Payzant had been ordained minister of Alline's old church on July 3, 1786, largely, it seems, in order to neutralize the impact of Methodism in the region.

When Garrettson returned to the United States, it was assumed by many that he would be appointed the general superintendent of Methodist missions in British North America and the West Indies, but for some reason or other, nothing came of this scheme. Instead, Garrettson continued to labor as an itinerant preacher, and for many years he served as the presiding elder of the New York district. He had a large estate at Rhinebeck, and he used his considerable wealth, further augmented by his marriage into the wealthy Livingston family, to support the Methodist cause, particularly in New York state. Until his death in 1827 Garrettson remained an ardent critic of the "crying sin" of slavery, an enthusiastic and committed disciple of John Wesley and an unreconstructed evangelical.[38]

Garrettson's quitting Nova Scotia on April 10, 1787, did not, it should be stressed, bring to an end the Methodist plan to assert their religious hegemony over the colony. Though not yet ordained, William Black and James and John Mann, Loyalists from New York, William Grandin, a New Jersey Loyalist, and "Old Moses," the Black Methodist preacher at Shelburne, continued to preach Wesley's gospel, supported briefly by James Oliver Cromwell, whose poor health compelled him to leave Nova Scotia in May. A year later two new Methodist missionaries arrived in the colony — William Jessop, the saintly Delaware itinerant, and James Wray, a somewhat stiff, austere and, some would say, overly caustic Englishman.[39] Wray was appointed by Wesley as "superintendent" of the work in Nova Scotia; it was a serious mistake. Within a year Wray, who was incapable of understanding North American Methodism, had resigned. In May of 1789 the Mann brothers and Black were ordained in Philadelphia. Black's ordination prepared the way for his being appointed Wray's replacement. Moreover, and this fact is extremely important, the three newly ordained Methodist ministers could now baptize and dispense communion and thus compete effectively with the two ordained New Lights, Payzant and Chipman, as well as with the more numerous Anglican ministers.

Jessop could almost fit Garrettson's shoes; he was a man "of powerful eloquence," who both preached and experienced sanctification.[40] However, he lacked Garrettson's enthusiasm for itinerating and lacked as well his energy; this significantly limited the impact Jessop had on late eighteenth century Nova Scotia. Nevertheless, Jessop effectively built upon Garrettson's work, especially in the Barrington area, and firmly established the Methodist cause there before his premature death in the United States in 1795.

By the beginning of the last decade of the eighteenth century, the

Methodists had four ordained ministers in Nova Scotia and a number of unordained itinerants. Five hundred and ten members were reported from the colony in official records[41] — unofficial records provide a somewhat higher number — and it seemed that the Methodists were on the verge of becoming the largest and most influential Protestant denomination in Nova Scotia and the organizational means whereby Alline's New Light–evangelical movement might have been channelled into oblivion.

In New Brunswick, Duncan McColl and hundreds of Methodist supporters were desperately looking for leadership and direction, but the Methodists had failed to take into account one important fact — the revival Garrettson had helped both to inspire and to shape had not only significantly revived the New Light movement, but it had also pushed to the surface a remarkable group of young, dynamic, committed and, some would say, "inspired" preachers. These men, men like Harris Harding, Joseph Dimock, James Manning, Theodore Seth Harding, would become the so-called "patriarchs" of the Nova Scotia and New Brunswick Baptist Church.

According to the 1827 Nova Scotia census, the New Light Baptist counteroffensive had been amazingly successful. The total population of Nova Scotia in 1827 was estimated at 142,548. This included 31,199 Anglicans, 42,060 Presbyterians, 31,882 Roman Catholics, 19,849 Baptists, 9,567 Methodists, 2,970 Lutherans and 5,042 others. The Baptist percentage in 1827 was 16 percent, and the Methodist 7.6 percent. By 1871 there were 73,295 Baptists, 18.9 percent of the total Nova Scotia population of 387,800, and 40,345 Methodists, 10.4 percent of the total. In New Brunswick, in 1861, 23 percent of the population was Baptist — almost 60,000 of the total population of 252,047, while 25,000 were Methodists — some 10 percent. Ten years later, in 1871, 25 percent of New Brunswickers were Baptists and 10 percent were still Methodists.[42]

Alline's disciples, in their nineteenth-century Baptist manifestation, whether Calvinist or Free Christian, had obviously won a decisive numerical victory over the Wesleyan Garrettsonians, and they had done so in an extremely difficult demographic environment. The Wesleyans, in my view, should have done better — much, much better — especially when both the Loyalist immigration and the growing strength of the British connection are taken into account.

III

Most of Yankee Nova Scotia, in a religious sense, had been assiduously cultivated by Alline and his disciples during the period immediately preceding Garrettson's arrival in the colony. Though most observers agreed with Alline that by early 1781 the "Great Awakening" had lost much of its earlier momentum in the Yankee heartland of the colony, he, Chipman, Bailey, Payzant and others continued to preach the New Light–evangelical gospel in the more peripheral areas of the region, such as the Saint John River Valley of what would become New Brunswick in 1784, and the South Shore of Nova Scotia. After Alline's death his three key disciples — Chipman, Bailey and Payzant — did not stop preaching, of course, but because each was now married, with family responsibilities, and they as a group lacked Alline's example and inspiration, they began to somewhat limit their itinerating. However, the Methodist offensive organized by Garrettson forced them to defend the Allinite–New Light legacy, and in the process, it should be stressed, their subsequent activities helped in bringing about the transformation of Alline's disorganized sect in Nova Scotia into the Baptist Church. Garrettson, it may be argued, did far more than any other individual in bringing about this transformation.

Garrettson was directly responsible for the conversion of three of the Nova Scotia New Light–Baptist "patriarchs" — Joseph Dimock, Harris Harding and Theodore Seth Harding. These three men, especially Harris Harding, were critically important human agents for bringing Edward Manning into the New Light–Baptist fold. Manning, without question, was the most important Maritime Baptist in the nineteenth century.[43]

Dimock was born in Newport, Nova Scotia, on December 11, 1768. His father was an active Baptist layman, and from his early youth Joseph Dimock received a well-grounded, basic biblical education from a distinctly Baptist perspective. At the age of seventeen, on July 17, 1785, he was — as he once put it — "born again" when "God the Spirit was pleased to strike my soul with terrors and amazement, so that I could find no rest until I was by the Spirit presented with the Saviour, his freeness and all-sufficiency to save all that came to him."[44] In this manner, while listening to the charismatic Freeborn Garrettson — who in so many respects was like Henry Alline — the teenage Dimock found his salvation.

Attracted by Garrettson's emphasis upon "free grace" and the transforming power of "regeneration," Dimock soon felt the need to preach the Christian gospel not only in Nova Scotia but also in neighboring New England and New York. Dimock was, indeed, a remarkable person. He possessed a "naturally affectionate disposition," and he was "one of the most amiable of men."[45] His associates often compared him to the apostle John "for his loving temper and gentleness of deportment." "There was no lordliness of spirit in him," it was stressed, "no arrogant assumptions and no demand for servile attention and homage."[46] Dimock was an excellent example for many of his contemporaries of a saintly man who had humbled himself, only to be exalted by the Almighty.

In September 1793 Dimock, after a long period itinerating, was ordained the minister of the Chester New Light church. He would remain a pastor of this church, which eventually became a Baptist church, until his death at the age of 79, in 1846. At his funeral service Dimock was, with good reason, described as a "good ... and wise man ... whose excellent disposition, engaging manner, integrity of heart, humility, and deep-toned piety, peculiarly fitted him for the work for which alone he seemed to live, and in the prosecution of which he died."[47]

One of Dimock's closest friends throughout his long life was Harris Harding — one of the most influential New Light Baptists of the 1790s and a person also converted during one of Garrettson's Nova Scotia revivals. According to one who knew him well, the Reverend I. E. Bill, Harris Harding's "pulpit talents ... intellectually considered, were never brilliant, but they were generally effective and useful."[48] Bill went on to describe perceptively what he considered to be the strengths and weaknesses of one of the Baptist "fathers":

> In the strictest sense, he was an extemporaneous preacher ... He deemed it of far more importance that the *heart* should be burning with love, than the *head* should be stored with matter ...
>
> If, in addressing a congregation, he never dazzled with the splendour of his eloquence, he often touched their sympathies, and moved their hearts as he descanted upon the Saviour's love ... At times there was a melting pathos in his utterances which was overpowering. While there was little method in his discourses, they were generally delivered with fervour, and interspersed with anecdotes illustrative of the topic he was discussing ... As regards religious zeal and activity, every day was devoted to God; and in this respect, his long life was one continuous Sabbath.[49]

The Reverend E. M. Saunders, the Nova Scotia Baptist author, commented in 1902 that "the dramatic power and element of personal magnetism were effective forces in the personality of the Reverend Harris

Harding. [He] skillfully spiced his anecdotes and conversation with a touch of comedy as natural to him as his breath. His imitations of people of peculiar speech were the delight especially of children."[50]

But to one who knew Harding at the beginning of his preaching career, there was little of redeeming value either in his character or in his preaching style. It was Simeon Perkins' contention in 1792 that Harding's "Extravagant Jestures & wild motions of his Body & hands, etc., is, to me very disgusting, and the pain he seems to be in Breath, is distressing."[51] The Liverpool merchant and general factotum and Methodist leader later maintained that "a man of his character and principles"[52] should never be permitted to preach the Christian gospel. Harding was, in Perkins' eyes, a dangerous antinomian who practised what he preached. For example, on September 28, 1796, Harding had been forced to marry — in Perkins' words — "a young woman [Hetty Huntington] said to be pregnant by him."[53]

For his biographer and co-minister at Yarmouth, the Reverend J. Davis, Harding was "an erratic genius."[54] He was "not in every sense a great man," and the "loftier reaches of argument and eloquence were beyond him":

> His utterance was ready, quick, overflowing, apt to be loud and vociferous — in his earlier days accompanied with much gesticulation and movement to and fro... Deep also was his pathos, abundant his unction, while his tears were frequent.
>
> Out of the pulpit he seemed to live by locomotion. Until arrested by his last sickness he was almost always on the road — alike on the move in winter as in summer... His capital was not so large as that of some other men; but he kept turning it over and over perpetually, until it had yielded an ample increase, and made its possessor "rich in good works"; superabundant in the fruits of his godly diligence.[55]

As far as his close associate the Reverend Theodore S. Harding was concerned, Harris Harding as a preacher was "not methodical":

> He dwelt most on the experimental part of religion, and greatly excelled in it. His great forte was "telling stories." He was full of anecdotes.
>
> He was eminently useful in the conversion of sinners perhaps more so than any man in this country. He would sometimes seem to

prophesy, and mark out people that he thought would be converted. He seemed to have an uncommon spirit of discernment that way.[56]

In 1854, the year Harding died, those who perhaps knew him best, the members of his Yarmouth congregation, described his long ministry in the community in the following manner:

> For nearly Seventy years, Sixty of which were spent in this neighborhood, he proclaimed the Gospel which he loved with unwearied diligence, and extraordinary success.
> "And they that be wise shall shine as the brightness of the firmament: and they that turn many to righteousness as the stars for ever and ever." Dan. 12:3.[57]

Harding had been born in Horton, Nova Scotia, on October 10, 1761, of Yankee Planter stock. Soon after his birth, his parents, like many other Nova Scotia Yankees, decided to return to Connecticut. During the early part of the American Revolutionary War, Harding, though only a teenager, evidently supported the Patriot side. He was arrested for a brief time by the British and imprisoned in a man-of-war. In 1783, despite his Patriot wartime activities, Harding (at the age of twenty-two) returned to the Horton region, where he became a schoolteacher. Though "a stranger to experimental religion" and "famous for his love of fun and frolic,"[58] Harding began to attend New Light services conducted by Payzant and Thomas Handley Chipman, the only ordained New Light preachers in Nova Scotia (after Alline left the province in August 1783). It should be noted that Harding, despite the fact that he became Alline's most enthusiastic advocate, never actually met the Falmouth preacher.

Harding not only attended New Light services, he also — in 1785, according to his sister — "was much taken up with the Methodists," especially Freeborn Garrettson. Garrettson, according to Harding's sister, had stressed that it was necessary for the individual to make "strenuous efforts in seeking the Lord." "Men must do their part," he declared, "and God would do his." Harding, as a result, attempted "to *work hard* for salvation instead of *believing heartily for it*."[59] He prayed no fewer than twelve times a day and he fasted every Friday, but despite this he could not "find his way into the heavenly kingdom." Instead of being part of "the great regenerating press," he found himself "plunged into despair."[60] When there appeared to be no hope, Thomas Handley Chipman nudged him in the New Light direction.

One "forenoon" in 1785, on his way to his schoolhouse, Harding "seemed all at once to obtain a view of Jesus." He realized — in retrospect at least — that "good works could not save him," but only his surrendering himself "to the Saviour, just as he was, to be saved 'freely by his grace,' and by that grace alone." When he arrived at his school, "joy and love transported his soul." His sister recalled that

> he forgot the children of his charge. Eternal glory was all before him, and he stood bathed in a flood of tears. His countenance was so altered, that the children gathered around him, they likewise in tears, and thought him dying. Truly there he began to live. When he came to his recollection he thought, by the sun on the window, that he must have been standing on one spot nearly an hour.[61]

Like Alline and like Garrettson, Harding had been "converted in a rapture" and "ever after he sought to live in a rapture" and he "judged ... his religious condition" and that of others by the intensity of their conversion experience.[62] Having had a traumatic conversion, Harding, like Alline and Garrettson, expected that everyone else should share the same emotional ecstasy and "the ravishing of the soul"[63] which he had experienced. Also like Alline and most of his disciples, Harding "placed great reliance on impressions, and often regarded them as direct intimations of the divine will, which it was his duty to obey."[64] For example, in 1790, while at Horton, Harding had a memorable dream "which much affected, and made a singular impression on his mind." "I dreamed," Harding wrote,

> I was on board a small sailboat, with deacon Cleaveland, and a number of my dear Christian friends at Horton. Methought I stood upon the gunwale of the boat, having a spear in my hand. The sun shone with peculiar brightness. We were running before a pleasant breeze, at a little distance from a delightful shore. The water also was clear as crystal, and I could see the white and shining fishes at the bottom, while I was continually catching them with the spear. My friends, I thought, were sitting speaking of Christ's love to a fallen world, their cheeks bathed with tears, and apparently filled with peace and joy. I thought the deacon said to me, "You catch every fish you strike." I replied, "I miss none." Methought I fished until I had got the boat filled and then had a delicious feast with my fellow-disciples. I awoke in a joyful frame. I visited Yarmouth soon after.[65]

The dream, according to Harding, was God's means of directing him to Yarmouth "to fish for men."

Harris Harding, if he had become a Methodist preacher, a Garrettsonian rather than an Allinite Baptist, would have significantly altered the shape of popular religion in the Maritimes. In all likelihood, Methodists would have outnumbered Baptists in Nova Scotia by the middle of the nineteenth century. Moreover, Methodism would have at its core an American New Light emphasis rather than a British sense of order and decorum.

Theodore Seth Harding was born in March 1773 at Barrington, Nova Scotia. His parents were Yankee Congregationalists. In 1781, soon after his father's death, the eight-year-old T. S. Harding first met Henry Alline when the Falmouth preacher "put his hand upon his head and prayed, May God be a father to this boy!" Apparently, the young Harding "trembled from head to foot, and at once felt deeply impressed with his need of a Saviour."[66] Six years later, in 1787, the fourteen-year-old Harding came under the influence of Freeborn Garrettson. "Liberty came to his soul" as he experienced the profound ecstasy of regeneration. After a short period of backsliding, when he mingled "in vain and worldly society," Harding's faith was revived "under the preaching of Joseph Dimock and Harris Harding" — who too had been brought to Christ largely through Garrettson's preaching.[67]

Instead of becoming a New Light Baptist, Harding, now in his early twenties, after a long discussion with William Black, resolved to become a Methodist itinerant like his hero Garrettson. Harding at this time, it should be stressed, considered himself to be a disciple of Freeborn Garrettson. Black sent Harding in 1793 to Horton — the New Light–Allinite centre — with the following instructions:

> You are going to the country to preach. You are a young man. It is a remarkable thing for so young a man to be in the ministry. You will be flattered, but remember, so surely as your pride is kindled, your usefulness is at an end. Besides, much that you hear will not be worth your regard. They will call you an angel to-day, and a devil to-morrow; when they pronounce you an angel, be not inflated; when a devil, be not depressed.[68]

After spending some two years in the Horton-Cornwallis area as a Methodist preacher, the impressionable Harding in late 1795 became an enthusiastic convert to the Calvinist-Baptist cause. Harding would throughout his career find it difficult to resist strong situational pressures. After his baptism in Halifax, Harding was ordained minister of the Horton Baptist church, and his "connection continued until dissolved by death in 1855."[69] On hearing of Harding's death, the Reverend I. E. Bill declared:

> Father Harding was a brilliant star in the bright constellation. In pulpit eloquence he excelled them all [that is the so-called Baptist Patriarchs]. In this department he was always popular with all classes, and continued so to the last. His appearance in the pulpit was commanding and dignified, his style bold and nervous, his scriptural quotations select and impressive, his imagination lively and active, his feelings deep and pungent, and his voice like the sound of a trumpet. For comprehensiveness of expression and readiness of utterance Father Harding was unequalled.[70]

Even more influential than Harding in the religious life of Nova Scotia in the pre-1860 period was Edward Manning — the so-called "Baptist Pope" of the Maritimes. Though not directly affected by Garrettson, Manning was certainly indirectly and significantly influenced by the Maryland Methodist because of the crucial role that Dimock and Harding played in Manning's conversion in 1789. Throughout the first half of the nineteenth century until his death in 1851, it should be stressed, Edward Manning was the most powerful single individual within the Nova Scotia Calvinist Baptist Church.[71]

If any one individual was responsible for channelling the New Light–Allinite/Free Will–Garrettsonian tradition into the Calvinist Baptist Church, it was Edward Manning. Reacting violently against his own New Light–Free Will past, Manning did everything in his power to ensure that the radical New Light legacy of the 1780s and early 1790s would atrophy into dark oblivion. Manning was evidently haunted by his Allinite and his Garrettsonian past, and he was determined to stamp his Baptist and Calvinist mark on his growing denomination.

Manning was physically imposing — well over six feet in height — and he was a powerful and persuasive preacher and a stubbornly determined individual. He was absolutely convinced that he knew what was best for his denomination, and he was determined to force his will upon his fellow Baptists. As the nineteenth century unfolded, especially in the post-1825 period, he pushed his often reluctant Baptist followers both in New Brunswick and Nova Scotia, but especially in the latter province, towards Anglo-American Calvinist order and away from New Light enthusiasm. This was, it may be argued, Manning's most significant contribution to the religious life of nineteenth-century Nova Scotia.

Born in 1766 in Ireland, Manning was still an infant when his parents moved to the Falmouth region of Nova Scotia. A decade before his conversion in 1789, Manning remembered Henry Alline's urging him "to flee from the wrath to come."[72] Soon after his conversion Manning began to itinerate throughout New Brunswick, Nova Scotia and northern Maine. A principal participant in Nova Scotia's manifestation of antinomianism — "the New Dispensation movement"[73] — Manning became disturbed with the divisive religious forces he had helped to unleash, and by the late 1790s he had become an ardent Calvinist. Gradually he used his position as pastor of the Cornwallis Baptist church to assert his authority over the growing Baptist denomination, first in the Annapolis Valley area and then throughout the entire Maritime region. He was an indefatigable busybody, interested in every aspect of denominational life, and he was at the crest of the Baptist wave as it swept across both Nova Scotia and New Brunswick in the 1820s and 1830s.

Garrettson's impact on the religious life of Nova Scotia may be perceived in a variety of ways. By examining it through the lens of his journal and his letters, a rather impressionistic picture emerges. There are hundreds of faceless Nova Scotians responding either positively or negatively to his evangelistic message. These people are largely frozen in time; they are lifeless and devoid of motivation. On the other hand, there is the collective biography of some of the Baptist patriarchs who were radically affected by the Garrettsonian revival. These men are certainly not lifeless, colorless and faceless Nova Scotians. They, too, provide a lens, however imperfectly ground, through which one can ascertain certain rough contours of a largely forgotten Canadian religious revival.

III

By 1799 only two American Methodist missionaries remained in Nova Scotia, and there was little enthusiasm in Methodist circles in the United States to increase that number. For a variety of reasons the British colony was seen in a negative light — as "Nova Scarcity"[74] — and, moreover, Bishop Asbury was not eager to send off his young itinerants to an alien land from which, he once noted, they returned to the United States "not so humble and serious as when they went."[75] Without American assistance, and without evangelical preachers of the Garrettson mould, the remaining Nova Scotia and New Brunswick Methodist preachers proved to be no match for the New Light Baptist itinerants. Native Nova Scotia and New Brunswick Methodist preachers like Black, John and James Mann and Duncan McColl were no match for the young, dynamic and — for many — charismatic Edward Manning, the Hardings, and Joseph Dimock and their increasing number of unusually gifted converts. By 1799, the evidence suggests, Black was a largely spent force — a man who had reached the peak of his influence in the 1780s but who experienced a steady but inexorable decline until the 1820s. John Mann, though very committed, was an ineffective preacher, and according to Simeon Perkins his "voice and Manner" were "uncooth."[76] Mann's brother, James, on the other hand, especially towards the end of his life in 1820 was "chaste, edifying, and usually unimpassioned," but in the 1790s — while still free to itinerate — he revealed a remarkable "lack of responsibility."[77] Duncan McColl (who died in 1830), though he was quite able, seldom strayed from the St. Stephen area of New Brunswick.

These four Methodist patriarchs shared a number of things in common. They were, according to Goldwin French, "more formal in their religious practice than their American brethren."[78] Moreover, as the nineteenth century unfolded, they also became increasingly obsessed with order and increasingly suspicious of New Light enthusiasm. Consequently, William Black was delighted to report in September 1804 that, unlike the Baptist New Lights, the Maritime Methodists were much "esteemed by those in authority for their quiet and orderly lives, good morals and strict loyalty."[79] The Maritime Methodists, in other words, using the New Light Baptists as a foil, were underscoring their own respectability and their own British roots; but in the process, and this point needs to be emphasized, they were cutting themselves off from most ordinary Nova Scotians, who simply wanted Allinite–New Light enthusiasm in their preachers. While the Maritime Methodists became increasingly dependent upon British Methodism for their paradigm of religious behavior, tens of thousands of New Brunswickers and Nova Scotians were looking to indigenous New Light Baptist preachers — people like themselves — who resonated with the popular religious culture of a rural society they knew so well.

For the Methodist elite in the late 1790s and first decades of the nineteenth century, religious enthusiasm led first to "fanaticism" and then to "infidelity."[80] For men like the Hardings, Dimock and Edward Manning and their growing number of followers, religious enthusiasm, the "workings of the Holy Spirit," was an unmistakable sign that what they referred to as a "Great Reformation" was actually occurring. It is not surprising, therefore, that one Nova Scotia Methodist leader felt compelled to complain in 1822 "because we oppose their enthusiastic excesses I do not permit people to rise up and speak, ... to rant and rave in our solemn assemblies ... they [the New Lights] would endeavour to persuade our people that they are in bondage."[81] In this one cogent statement the Reverend Robert Alder, a recently arrived British Methodist, summed up why, by the 1820s, the Methodists had been displaced by the Baptists as the most influential evangelical denomination in southern Nova Scotia and New Brunswick. By rejecting so much of their Garrettsonian legacy, the Maritime Methodists at a critical juncture in the history of the region, had enabled the New Light Baptists — both Free Will and Calvinist — to overtake them in terms of numbers and societal influence.

It would be a serious mistake, however, to conclude that the Garrettsonian legacy was of no consequence to nineteenth- and twentieth-century Maritime Methodism. It is noteworthy that Methodism remained relatively strong in those regions of Nova Scotia where Garrettson exerted his greatest influence in his all too brief sojourn in Nova Scotia. There is therefore a sharp ring of truth in the observation made by R. D. Simpson in 1984 that "Garrettson's impact upon Nova Scotia was almost equal to that of Wesley in Great Britain and Ashbury in the United States."[82] Had Garrettson stayed longer — here the historian must stop — I am certain that the religious landscape of the Maritimes would have been radically different in the nineteenth and the twentieth centuries.[83]

Chapter IV

From Newlight to Baptist: Harris Harding and the Second Great Awakening in Nova Scotia

I

Contemporaries called the remarkable outburst of religious enthusiasm which engulfed much of Nova Scotia in 1806, 1807 and 1808 "the Great Reformation."[1] It was not referred to as a mere revival of religion but rather in terms which William G. McLouglin has used to describe intense revitalization movements.[2] It was regarded as being more than a revival; and it was. It was perhaps the most spectacular outward manifestation of one of the most important social movements in nineteenth-century Nova Scotia history — the so-called "Second Great Awakening." A principal actor in the unfolding drama of the "Second Great Awakening" as well as a crucial human link connecting important aspects of Henry Alline's New Light movement with the evolving Nova Scotia Calvinist Baptist Church was the controversial Nova Scotia preacher, Harris Harding.

It is of some interest that so much has been written about Nova Scotia's First Great Awakening and relatively little about the Second Great Awakening. The Second Great Awakening, it may be argued, stretched from 1790 to 1812 — from the afterglow of the Garrettson revival to the outbreak of the War of 1812. There were a number of local revivals in the early period and a more general revival at the turn of the century. Then came "the Great Reformation" of 1806, 1807 and 1808 — the remarkable culmination of the earlier revivals — the spiritual and emotional peak of the revitalization movement. This was followed by a number of isolated revivals, and then there was a period of declension overlapping with the War of 1812.

The First Great Awakening has received a great deal of scholarly attention for three major reasons. First, it occurred at the time of the American Revolution, and since so many historians are, and have been, very interested in the Revolution, some have understandably focused their attention on the relationship of the Awakening to Nova Scotia's enigmatic response to the Revolution. Second, the First Great Awakening owed a great deal to a single charismatic leader — Henry Alline — who left to posterity a journal, over 500 hymns, a number of sermons and two major treatises. Alline has attracted scholars like a giant magnet, and with good reason. Third, some attention has been drawn to Nova Scotia's First Great Awakening because of what to many is the continuing scholarly preoccupation with New England's First Great Awakening and the relative paucity, until recently, of serious studies dealing with New England's Second Great Awakening.[3]

Nova Scotia's First Great Awakening has been perceived in a variety of ways by different historians and scholars. For Maurice Armstrong, the religious revival was simply a "retreat from the grim realities of the world to the safety and pleasantly exciting warmth of the revival meeting, and to profits and rewards of another character."[4] According to S. D. Clark, it was basically a "reflection of the collapse of the traditional leadership of the Nova Scotia village communities and the development of a great mass movement of social protest" against the colony's capital, Halifax. The Great Awakening, in other words, was an outsettlement democratic protest "against traditionalism, against authority."[5] For J. M. Bumsted, the "Great Awakening of Nova Scotia was principally a movement of spiritual reform much like those which had over the centuries convulsed Christendom."[6] And as far as Gordon Stewart and I have been concerned, Alline's Awakening was the means whereby many confused and disoriented Nova Scotians resolved their collective identity crisis during the American Revolutionary War.[7] But Alline, according to some of my most recent work, also operated at another level of understanding. Alline preached "the simple, emotional Evangelical gospel of the 'New Birth' and thus provided a powerful new personal and spiritual relationship between Christ and the redeemed believer in a world where all traditional relationships were falling apart."[8]

It seems obvious that each of these interpretations, or a combination of them, could also be applied to the Second Great Awakening. Yet there are certain dangers in looking for sophisticated explanations of a complex event before that event is understood even at a most elementary or rudimentary level. What is first necessary is to discern in as sensitive and sophisticated a manner as possible the essential anatomy of the Awakening. It is essential to come to grips with the chronology of events and the personalities and issues involved. Once this is done, a few possible explanations may be put forward — but even then they must be advanced in a hesitant and almost reluctant manner.

II

On December 5, 1806, the Reverend Thomas Handley Chipman, the influential New Light Baptist minister from the Annapolis region and an ardent disciple of Henry Alline, reported to the readers of the *Massachusetts Baptist Missionary Magazine* that he had been in the Yarmouth-Argyle region for five weeks and that "such glorious times I never saw before." "Multitudes are turned to God," he observed. "I cannot with ink and pen . . . describe the one half God has done." Chipman went on:

> Since the work began (three months ago), there have been about one hundred and fifty souls brought to own Jesus, as their rightful Lord and sovereign king . . . We have had two church meetings, and surely I never saw such meetings before. It was indeed the house of God, and the very gate of heaven. The last Saturday we began at ten in the morning, and continued until eight in the evening, to hear persons relate the dealings of God with their souls, and then a great number were prevented for want of time . . .
>
> A great many of the subjects of this work have been young people and children. Seldom a meeting but some are brought to embrace the offers of life; sometimes five, six, and seven at a meeting. There are meetings in some parts of the town almost every day.[9]

Late in January 1808 the Reverend Harris Harding, who had played a key role in triggering the "Great Reformation," also wrote to the *Massachusetts Baptist Missionary Magazine.* Harding observed that "previous to the Lord's pouring upon us the gracious effusions of his Holy Spirit there had been a great declension in religion, attended with great discouragement of souls in believers, and coldness, backwardness, and neglect of religious duties."[10] "Since the fifth of October last," he went on, "140 persons" had been baptized and "upwards of two hundred persons have been savingly united in Christ."[11] What is remarkable is that the estimated total population of the immediate Yarmouth area was only 1,000, and of this number, some, of course, were Acadian Roman Catholics, and others, staunch Anglicans.

Harding pointed out that "God has also been pleased to revive his gracious work" to the east of Yarmouth, in the townships of "Argyle and Barrington."[12] It was a region which Harding had frequently visited, and he was understandably delighted when his close friend, the Reverend Enoch Towner, could report on April 13, 1807, that in the autumn of the previous year "the Lord had begun his work" in Argyle. As had been the experience in Yarmouth and would also be the case in other areas of Nova Scotia, the early momentum in the "awakening" was provided by teenagers and some who were even younger. According to Towner,

> the young professors manifested a desire to follow their Lord's commands and to be buried with him in baptism... I was at a loss how to proceed, but resolved... to hear their experiences... Nine... [including] seven young converts were baptized... After this the work spread with great power, and people assembled from all parts of the town... I thought it proper to send for brother Harris Harding... as he had formerly laboured among them... ten came forward and were baptized. We both went into the water together, to show that we agreed in heart and practice. The glory of the Lord seemed to overshadow the place, and move on the baptismal waters.[13]

From July 1806 to late October, Towner baptized over 100 people. Then, in the early months of 1807 he noticed that the "divine presence" had once again "filled the place — many giving glory to their Redeemer, and many deeply wounded with a sense of their sins." Towner concluded his report by stressing that

> the last Sabbath in March twenty came forward and were baptized. There were five baptisms in the winter season. Twenty-four have told their experiences, who are not yet baptized, and a number of others are under hopeful impressions. The work is still going on in this place, and spreading rapidly in different parts of this province.[14]

One of these "different parts" was Liverpool, a settlement where the Baptists were weak but where the New Lights — Henry Alline's followers — had always been strong and where, moreover, Harding had spent many months over the years preaching the New Light gospel. In March 1807 the Reverend John Payzant, the only ordained New Light minister in Nova Scotia, who had stubbornly refused to become a Baptist, noted that a number of women and young people on the geographical periphery of

Liverpool had experienced conversion and were moving from "House to House and telling what great [things] the Lord had done for them." There were nightly meetings and the "young people" were especially active, but the Reverend Payzant was not at all involved at this early stage — in what he described as "a wonderfully moving [among the people] of the power of God." Finally, on March 3, what Payzant referred to as "the fire" began "to kindle" and "the flame" engulf his Meeting House:

> At night meeting... as soon as the Sermon was ended the people began to Shout from all sides of the House, either Crying for mercy under a Since [sense] of their parishing condition; or rejoicing and blessing God, for his Goodness to them. The Sinners were cut down by the all mighty power of God, under a Since that they were in a ruined condition, and the Lord has appeared for a number of them, their language was the Lord has appeared and delivered my soul, he has made an everlasting covenant with my Soul. I shall reign with him to all eternity... and as soon as any one came out, they would call to others to come and partake with them, telling them that there was mercy for them, for they had been the worst of Sinners. And acknowledging all their bad deeds, and if there were any person that they had anything against, they were the first that they went to, and asked their pardon, all offences were made up, and the meeting continued till day. The number that experienced the love of God on their hearts are not yet ascertained. There were more than 20 that came out clear; but it is thought by Some that Stade all night, that there was more than 50 who experienced the love of God.
>
> The next day, by the break of day, the Streets were full of people, of all descriptions, and it appeared that there was ten times as many people in the place as before. So it continued all day they going from house to house. There was no business done that week and but little victuals dressed. The people were So many for there was old and young, rich and poor, male and female, Black and White, all met together and appeared to be as one. At night they came into the meeting House in that manner; the meeting House echo'd with their Praises and rejoicing. So that there was no publick Singing or Prayers but the whole night was Spent in that manner. It was judged that there was above 1000 people.

After the meeting the assembled throng went from house to house. They were led by "many Small Boys and Girls, Some of them telling the goodness of God, others in distress." Exhausted, conscience-stricken, introspective yet enjoying their unexpected influence and power, the young inhabitants of Liverpool continued to witness during the day and to meet together at night. The adults at the evening meeting complained of the constant noise and the yelling. They wanted to hear sermons and, moreover, they demanded order. The young refused to abandon what they considered to be practices sanctioned by the Holy Spirit.

At the end of March 1807, forty-four joined the church. "More than 1000 people" attended that special service. The entire next week "was spent in having meetings, every night, the young people meet[ing] in various places, for they were too numerous to meet in one place." "When-ever a number of them met together," it was noted, "the time was spent Singing Hymns and praying."[15]

The meetings continued until August, when Harris Harding arrived. Harding obviously wanted to make Baptists of all the new converts. Payzant vociferously opposed the move, and the "Reformation" was replaced by bitter sectarian strife. Some — according to Payzant — were "dipped in bitter water for Baptism." "It appeared," he spitefully main-tained, "that they thought [that] to dip people in water was all the religion that was needful."[16]

At Chester the Reverend Joseph Dimock noted in his journal that in August 1807

> the Lord made a glorious descent upon the earth against the strong-holds of sin and Satan, and caused a great shaking among the dry bones, and bone came to his bone, so that the Sabbath on which the work broke out was concluded with a great shout among the saints, and a great outcry among sinners for mercy... Our meetings are large, for people throng in great abundance from every quarter to hear.

On the first Sunday in October, twenty people were baptized, including Dimock's wife. Fourteen were baptized on the next two Sundays, and by late November "more than forty" had been baptized — "both old and young, male and female."[17]

It is noteworthy that the revitalization movements in Yarmouth, Argyle, Liverpool and Chester owed so much to Harris Harding. Over the years he had carefully cultivated this area, and in 1806 and 1807 what was commonly referred to as "the rich harvest of souls" was finally reaped. But in other regions of Nova Scotia considerable life was breathed into the movement by visiting Massachusetts Calvinist Baptist preachers like Isaac Case, Daniel Merrill, Henry Hale and Amos Allen. Spurred by the events of the Second Great Awakening in New England and inspired by what they knew was occurring in Yarmouth and Argyle, these Yankee Baptists in late 1807 brought what they called "a reformation" to the Baptist heartland located at Horton and Cornwallis and also to the Onslow and Cumberland regions of Nova Scotia. They also brought with them the conviction that Nova Scotia's Second Awakening would be, for Baptists, as ephemeral as the First unless every means available was used to impose on it a firm Calvinist Baptist organizational form — one eagerly appropriated from Massachusetts.

It seems clear that the "Great Reformation" was of considerable importance in consolidating the position of the Calvinist Baptist Church in Nova Scotia in particular and the Maritime region in general. The revitalization movement provided the means whereby the revivalistic paradigm first articulated and applied by Henry Alline was appropriated by the Nova Scotia Baptists. In other words, the New Light traditions, significantly shaped by new events and personalities, became the Calvinist Baptist heritage and the means whereby the Nova Scotia Baptist patriarchs hoped to impose their religious hegemony over Yankee Nova Scotia. Considerable light is shed on this often complex process of transformation by an examination of the fascinating early life and career of Harris Harding.

III

Harding, as has already been pointed out, was born in Horton, Nova Scotia, on October 10, 1761, of Yankee pre-Loyalist stock. Soon after his birth his parents returned to Connecticut, but in 1783, at the age of twenty-two, and despite his pro-Patriot wartime activities, Harris Harding returned to the Horton area with his father. Harding became a school teacher and also attended local New Light services conducted by the Reverend John Payzant, Henry Alline's brother-in-law.

In 1783 Payzant and Thomas Handley Chipman were the only ordained New Light preachers in Nova Scotia, aside from Alline; and on the latter's death in 1784, each regarded himself as Alline's logical successor. Payzant would always be opposed to the Baptists, regarding adult baptism — as had Alline — as a "non essential." Chipman, on the other hand, had been baptized by immersion in 1779 soon after he had been converted by Alline.

If any one man attempted to push the New Light movement in the direction of the Baptist Church in the latter part of the eighteenth century, it was Chipman. He could do it because Nova Scotians knew that he was one of Alline's closest associates; he had crisscrossed the colony with the Falmouth evangelist. Chipman had, in a sense, been legitimized by Alline's success and friendship. He struggled long and hard with Payzant to protect the New Lights from antinomian "New Dispensationalism," and then when this was accomplished, he turned against Payzant in order to create a tightly knit Calvinist yet evangelical Baptist Church. For Chipman, Baptist Church order was the one available organizational means whereby the Nova Scotia New Light tradition could be effectively channelled into evangelical respectability, and Alline's sometimes anarchic sectarianism into denominationalism.

Harding was evidently converted sometime in 1785 in the midst of one of the myriad of Garrettson's revivals. He had a extraordinary conversion experience, and he expected that everybody else should share at the individual level the same emotional ecstasy and the "ravishing of the soul" which he had experienced, as well as the white heat of the community revival.[18] Soon after his conversion, Harding accompanied Payzant in March 1786 to Chester, where Harding served as the minister's special exhorter.

Harding's role as an exhorter for a more experienced minister was certainly not unique but was rather a common feature of Nova Scotia revivalism in the post-Alline period. Exhortation — a complex mix of personal testimony, introspective prayer, the singing of some of Alline's hymns — became a vitally important ingredient in Nova Scotia's Second Great Awakening. The preacher — a person like Payzant — would base his extemporaneous sermon on a verse of Scripture; and for an hour or so as he developed his argument, various people in his congregation, young and old, male and female, rich and poor, sensitive and insensitive, bright and stupid, were compelled to confront in a general, almost impersonal, manner the inevitability of death, the eternal reality of heaven and hell, the need for salvation and the crucial role played by Christ in linking the redeemed sinner to the omniscient and omnipotent Almighty. This kind of extemporaneous preaching helped to create a mood of anticipation; it also helped to focus the attention of the congregation on those spiritual issues which preoccupied preachers like Payzant. To personalize these issues and to drive the jagged edges of their stark reality into the "minds and hearts" of the listeners, a special time of "exhortation" was always set aside at the end of each sermon. Not only was the sermon personalized by the exhorter, it was also carefully carved up and parts of it were aimed explicitly at specific people in the congregation — at friends, neighbors and associates, or at enemies, strangers and the curious.[19]

Exhorting was also a time for testing a possible preacher of the New Light gospel. It is clear then that in Chester, Payzant was in fact testing Harding — to see whether he truly possessed the spirit of the Almighty and was genuinely called to follow in the footsteps of Alline and Garrettson. Payzant was a little concerned about his protégé: when he wandered off "with some of old acquaintance . . . he had gone with a bad crew." Payzant pointed out in his journal that he saw "what a danger [Harding] was in if he gave way to the enemy and Satan like a Roving Lion seeking whom he may devour."[20]

But Harding was not devoured — at least not in the way Payzant had feared. He soon began to itinerate on his own — to Liverpool in 1787, to Chester in 1788, throughout Annapolis County in 1789, to Onslow, Yarmouth and Amherst in 1790 and back to Liverpool in 1791, and to Shelburne, Barrington, Argyle and Yarmouth.[21] On his travels Harding did everything in his power to emulate Henry Alline — who by 1790 had become his role model. Harding tried to look like Alline — according to one contemporary observer, "his form was slender, frail, and even ghostly."[22] In later life, however, Harding became quite corpulent: "His length and breadth seemed to be so nearly equal as to suggest ideas of the square and cubical."[23] Harding, moreover, tried to preach Alline's gospel. As far as Simeon Perkins was concerned — and he had often heard Alline — Harding's "Doctrines are much the Same as was propagated by Mr. Alline."[24] Not only did Harding try to cultivate Alline's preaching style and physical image, he even gave the impression at times that he too was dying from consumption.

Harding also used many of Alline's techniques as well as carefully visiting those areas where Alline had been successful. Harding, for example, used Alline's hymns, and he often explicitly appealed to women and children.[25] He even attempted to use Alline's imagery and language and wrote many letters to his friends in Horton and Cornwallis, hoping that these letters would eventually be published — thus making him famous.[26] To Thaddeus Harris, for example, he observed from Annapolis on May 14, 1789:

> The Mighty God of Jeshurun has girded his sword upon his thigh, and is riding in the flaming chariot of Israel like a glorious Conqueror: his majesty and power are seen amongst the inhabitants of Annapolis. Some have of late felt his dying groans reach their

despairing souls . . . I see again the immortal shore that flows with milk and honey . . .[27]

Harding was determined, as he graphically put it in 1791, to "go in the name of brother Alline's God."[28] When asked once about the publication of his letters "to the Christians," he could only answer — as he put it — "with dear dear brother Alline, God forbid I should write or speak anything but what I would publish, if possible, over the four quarters of the globe."[29] From the declining Loyalist centre of Shelburne he wrote to Thaddeus Harris on August 23, 1791:

> O brother, stand in that gospel that Henry Alline once proclaimed to your soul, and others in Cornwallis. That is the gospel that is the life of my soul, and if I am called to it will not only suffer for, but seal with my blood.[30]

Two days later Harding was planning to follow Alline to New England. He asserted, "Sometimes I can see a man stand and call, 'Come over and help us.' I assuredly believe God has called me to preach the gospel on the other side of the flood."[31] But Harding never made his way to New England. Instead he had to be satisfied with — as he put it — "shaking . . . the dry bones"[32] in southern Nova Scotia and in writing to Alline's brother in Falmouth. It was a strange, yet characteristic, letter:

> The lowing of the milch kine is heard in this land. The angel of the Lord is riding on the white horse through Barrington. Three are converted; numbers under great distress, groaning for mercy; and almost every soul is shocked through the place. Jesus also spreads his blessed wings over Argyle; his kingdom is come into three souls in that place, of late, and several are waiting heavily under their guilt. The saints frequently in meeting are crying aloud, 'The sword of the Lord and of Gideon' and righteousness breaks in like an overflowing flood into our Assemblies.[33]

Harding could hardly contain his delight when he was told by one Nova Scotian in 1791 that his preaching was precisely "the Gospel that brought salvation to my soul under Henry Alline."[34]

In common with many of his close associates, Harding "placed great reliance on impressions, and often regarded them as direct intimations of the divine will, which it was his duty to obey."[35] Often he regarded his wish and desire to be the explicit command of the Holy Spirit. It is not surprising, therefore, that Harding became a central figure in the New Dispensation movement in Nova Scotia which significantly affected the New Light movement in the last decade of the eighteenth century. At the core of the movement were to be found Harris Harding, Joseph Dimock, and James and Edward Manning.[36] According to Edward Manning, after he had abandoned New Dispensationalism:

> Mr. Alline's lax observance of divine institutions fostered in the minds of his followers such ideas as these; that the ordinances are only circumstantials, outward matters, and mere non-essentials; that the scriptures are not the only rule of faith and practice; and that no person is under any obligation to perform any external duty until God immediately impresses the mind so to do ... Several began to question the propriety of having anything to do with external order or ordinances, and soon refused to commune with the church ... As they had no rule to go by but their fancies, which they called 'the Spirit of God,' great irregularities ensued.[37]

In May 1791 the New Dispensation movement took organizational form and ideological shape in Horton. It was an experience that the Reverend John Payzant would never forget. He noted in his journal:

> The Second Sabbath of May it was the turn to have the Church Meeting and Sacrament at Horton. Mrs. R. rose against all the orders of the Church and [said] that they were but outward forms and contrary to the Spirit of God. These novelties in the Church caused many to follow the same examples, which made trouble in the Church ... She told me that she had seen the Spirit of God, that baptism and the Lord'[s] Supper, with all Discipline of the Church, was contrary to the Spirit of God and his Gospel, and that marriage was from the Devil, that she was determined to live separately from her husband, for it was as much sin for her to have children by him [as] by any other man and she said that there [were] many that would follow her.[38]

By August the New Light Church was badly split — "all" was "in Confusion." The supporters of what Payzant called these "fantastical notion[s]" soon "spread from town to town and many adopted this new scheme."[39] The main propagator of New Dispensationalism was Harris

Harding, but he was ably assisted by the Mannings and Joseph Dimock. Seeing that the New Dispensationalists were threatening to destroy his church at Annapolis, the Reverend Thomas Handley Chipman, unlike Payzant, proposed a quick counteroffensive. He wanted all the New Dispensationalists expelled immediately from the two churches. Chipman felt that unless this was done, the New Light Church and the entire Allinite movement would quickly disintegrate into warring, bitter factions. Payzant had little enthusiasm for spiritual battle. He was satisfied with waiting for events to determine the future flow of spiritual development in the province, and he escaped to Liverpool in 1793 to get away from the troublemakers in his church. Chipman, on the other hand, went on the offensive. He was determined — as Simeon Perkins cogently expressed it — "to counteract the Antinomian doctrines that have been propagated in this Town [Liverpool] and other parts of the Province, principally... by Mr. Harris Harding."[40]

By late 1793 it was clear that the New Dispensation movement had peaked in Nova Scotia and was on the decline, especially in the Horton-Cornwallis region. The Mannings and Joseph Dimock had been frightened and appalled by the antinomian excesses practised by many of their former associates. Moreover, the disorder and chaos which seemed endemic to the movement appeared to threaten the already fragile underpinnings of Alline's movement. Short-term ecstasy was one thing; permanent confusion and disorientation were something else. The Baptist church polity advocated by T. H. Chipman became increasingly attractive. Joseph Dimock, who had been baptized by immersion in 1787, was ordained a minister of the Chester New Light church on September 10, 1793.[41] It was an ordination endorsed by Chipman and Payzant. Then, in the following year, Harding was ordained in a controversial ceremony as minister of the Onslow church by his close friend Dimock.[42] Neither Chipman nor Payzant felt able to participate in the ceremony since they felt — as Payzant put it — that Harding "had spoke much against ordination, against ordained Ministers, against the orders of the Church, and many Such like Things."[43] Harding, in other words, was an unreconstructed New Dispensationalist and unworthy of the Christian ministry.

Edward Manning, who was converted in May 1789, was ordained on October 19, 1795, as minister of the Cornwallis New Light church.[44] After spending some time in Maine with Calvinist Baptist preachers, and under great pressure from his brother James and Thomas Handley Chipman, Edward was baptized in 1797 by Chipman.[45] A year earlier James Manning had been baptized by Chipman as well; James Manning was ordained two years later.[46] The other "father" of the Nova Scotia Baptist Church, Theodore Seth Harding, was baptized on May 31, 1795, and ordained at the age of twenty-three in the following year.[47]

According to Theodore Harding, the Horton revival of 1799 "spread all down till it reached Yarmouth and then Harris Harding joined the Baptists."[48] Harris Harding had first visited Yarmouth in 1790, largely in response to a vivid dream.[49] The Reverend Jonathan Scott, Alline's formidable foe, was still at Chebogue; he would not leave the province for New England until 1793.[50] While in the Yarmouth region in 1792, Harding helped articulate into existence a revival of religion. There was, he reported on January 27, 1792, "a little cloud, like the bleeding hand of Jesus, in this part of the vineyard." By April, "near fifty . . . are savingly born again."[51]

While the revival fires were dampened in Yarmouth, Harding moved on to Liverpool. There were obviously souls to "catch" all along the Atlantic shore. The following year Harding was in the Cobequid region, leading a revival there. Then in 1794, as has been previously mentioned, he was ordained at Onslow. The following year he was on the move again, and in 1796 he was in Liverpool. Finally, on May 19, 1797, a distraught Onslow church "ordered a letter to be sent to call Rev. Harris Harding home."[52] But Harding refused to leave Yarmouth. He had, in all likelihood, moved there from Liverpool late in 1796. In the early months of 1796 Harding had played a key role in bringing about what Perkins called "a remarkable Stir of Religious Concern among people."[53] There was an "Extraordinary stir among the Young People, principally the Females." There were, according to Perkins, much "Swooning and Extices [ecstasies]."[54] Harding was exhilarated by the experience; he spent a great deal of time with the young people in the community, and some of the young women developed "a great natural fondness for him and thought all his tender expressions for [their] souls was the effect of natural passion."[55] Many young women had felt the same way about Henry Alline. They were sexually and spiritually attracted to men of vigor, decisiveness and élan.

In his relationship with one young woman, however, Harding went beyond the accepted norms of behavior. Perhaps he was, as Payzant suggested, merely putting into practice his antinomian beliefs, or it may have been that he was trapped into a marriage by a scheming Hetty Harrington.[56] All that is certain is that under strong community pressure Harding publicly confessed that he had impregnated the girl, and on September 28, 1796, he married her. Six weeks later a child was born to the couple.[57] Harding's supporters, who had wished him to replace Payzant, now withdrew their support, and early in 1797 Harding was called to the Yarmouth church. He continued to preach at Liverpool in 1797, but only in private houses.[58] He obviously still had his supporters, who were willing to forgive a man who was a sinner like themselves but also one who seemed to be a human conduit for the Holy Spirit.

IV

In Yarmouth, Harding "kept school for the support of his family."[59] Influenced by growing Baptist support in other regions of the province and under considerable pressure from old friends like the Mannings and Dimock, Harding was finally baptized by James Manning on August 28, 1799.[60] A revival was then sweeping through Yarmouth, and Manning had "been sent for to assist in the work." Manning described Harding's baptism in the following graphic manner:

> At the time the ordinance of baptism was administered the people looked as solemn as the grave. Mr. Harding's coming to the water seemed like Christ coming to Jordan. After he came from the water he prayed with the people in the street. It seemed as though he had a double portion of the Spirit. Some of the dear christians broke forth in praises to God and the Lamb...[61]

The revival of 1799–1800, although centred at Horton, radiated in all directions — up into the Saint John River Valley, into Cumberland, down the Annapolis Valley to Yarmouth and into Argyle and Barrington. It was obviously a Baptist revival. There was therefore a great deal of truth in Bishop Charles Inglis's report to the S.P.G. (Society for the Propagation of the Gospel) in which he warned of "the prevalence of an enthusiastic and dangerous spirit among a sect in the Province called New Lights, whose religion seems to be a strange jumble of New England independence and Behmenism. Formerly they were Pedobaptists, but by a recent illumination, they have adopted the Anabaptist scheme, by which their number has been much increased and their zeal enflamed."[62] Inglis was particularly concerned with Harris Harding's impact. According to the bishop, intelligence from the Yarmouth area stressed that

> a rage for dipping or total immersion prevails all over the western counties of the Province, and is frequently performed in a very

indelicate manner before vast collections of people. Several
hundreds have already been baptized, and this plunging they deem
to be absolutely necessary to the conversion of their souls. On the
Saturday preceding these solemnities the preacher sits above the
congregation with a number of select brethren on lower benches
appointed to assist him.[63]

Inglis also charged that the Baptist leaders were "engaged in a general plan
of total revolution in religion and civil government."[64] Clearly there was
no substantiation for this charge or for Inglis's contention that the Baptist
preachers were greatly influenced by the work of Thomas Paine.

The Anglican bishop, despite some of the glaring inaccuracies in his
report, had nevertheless correctly perceived the important transformation
of many New Lights into Baptists. Concerned about the need for order
and discipline, Payzant, the Mannings and Thomas Handley Chipman
met in July 1797 and agreed "to walk together in fellowship as ministers of
Jesus Christ" and "to hold a yearly conference, to know our minds, and
the state of the different churches standing in connection, by their delegates being sent by them."[65] In June 1798 the conference took place at
Cornwallis. According to Edward Manning's minutes:

> Mr. Handley Chipman spoke concerning the nature of an Associa-
> tion . . . Met again at five o'clock. Discoursed largely upon the neces-
> sity of order and discipline in the churches, and continued until
> midnight in observing the dangerous tendency of erroneous princi-
> ples and practices, and lamenting the unhappy consequences in our
> churches.[66]

Harris Harding requested admission to the conference. It was pointed out
that he had "deeply fallen into errors" by continuing to espouse the cause
of New Dispensationalism. Harding "professed sorrow, humbly acknowl-
edged his offences, signed a document to that effect, craved forgiveness of
his brethren, and was received."[67]

Sometime in 1799 the Reverend Thomas Handley Chipman visited
Boston to confer with the Reverend Samuel Stillman, the minister of the
First Baptist Church in Boston, about the suit brought against the Reverend Enoch Towner for conducting an illegal marriage in Nova Scotia.
Chipman was also in Boston, collecting ammunition for his final assault
on the decaying outworks of the New Light Church. Under Stillman's
considerable influence, Chipman saw the desperate need in Nova Scotia

for firm, Calvinist, Baptist denominational control. At the annual conference held in 1800 Chipman therefore presented "a close Baptist communion plan."[68] The Reverend John Payzant was furious. When he confronted Chipman, the Annapolis preacher replied "that Mr. Towner had been sued for Marrying and in order to defend the suit he had adopted that plan, that they might be called by some name for they were looked upon as nobody."[69] As Baptists, they would have some status in the community; they could stress their link with "the Danbury Association in New England."[70] Without this link and without the name they were without power and influence. It was proposed that the Association name be changed from "Congregational and Baptist" to "The Nova Scotia Baptist Association."[71] The Mannings, Dimock, Chipman, the Hardings and Towner, Joseph Crandall from New Brunswick — but not Payzant — accepted their certificates as members of the Baptist Association. It was then agreed by the Baptist ministers present that

> as many aspersions are cast upon the churches of Christ and the ministers of the gospel, for erroneous principles, etc., the associated ministers and messengers judge it expedient that our church articles of faith and practice should be printed, and the Churches in connection should defray the expense of printing said articles, and the plan of the Association.[72]

A key section of Alline's sect, in a sense, had in 1800 become the Nova Scotia Calvinist Baptist Church.

Chipman's Baptist yoke never rested easily on Harding's shoulders. He resented the growing pressure to exclude from communion those who had not been baptized by immersion as adults. He was willing, however, to accept the 1802 Association resolution "that the ordinance of Baptism should not be administered to any but those that join the Churches, except in cases where they cannot be blessed with such a privilege."[73] Harding, it is clear, was not all that interested in Association politics. He was more concerned in 1805 and 1806 with the fact that "the religious aspect in Yarmouth was sadly dark." He must also have been worried about the arrival in 1806 of the Reverend Ranna Cossit, an Anglican minister from Sydney. Cossit was well known as a person who appealed to "the 'lower class' of people."[74] Harding needed some convincing proof that he was indeed doing God's work in Yarmouth. He was thinking about abandoning the ministry unless his "commission . . . were sealed afresh with tokens of success."[75] He therefore decided to *will* into existence "The Great Reformation":

Under a strong presentiment of approaching blessing, he ventured to employ language like this: — "Sinners! I have long entreated you to repent and believe. But now I tell you God, by his Spirit, is coming to convince you of sin, of righteousness, and of judgment to come, and convert your souls. Fight against him much longer you cannot; or the Lord never spoke to me, nor by me — I am a deceiver, and deceived."[76]

Harding — like Alline — was able to use the spoken word as a "bare and brutal engine"[77] against the head and heart of his hearers. His sermons, it was noted, "abounded with short pithy sayings, such as are apt to stick to the memory like burs."[78] There is apparently only one extant verbatim excerpt from one of his early sermons, but this excerpt must have been characteristic of most of his sermons:

We don't always criticize as heaven will by and by. — The holiness of God is the sinner's torment. — A natural man can no more see beauty in Christ, than a blind man can in colours. — If Christ is anywhere, he is in the converted soul. — Heaven is a change of nature. — True faith is not in the head, but in the heart. — To meet with Christ is more than all the meetings in the world. — Christ in the ordinance makes it sweet. — Christians do more ofttimes to scatter souls from Christ than the unconverted do. — Where there's no love, there's no grace. I am going down to the grave. Blessed be God! There is a crown of faith laid up for them that love him. — Unbelief is the worst sin that a man can commit. — If God loves you, he loves you unchangeably. He does not love you for your frames and feelings; he loves you for his name's sake. — If you don't love holiness, you don't love God.[79]

At the start of a typical sermon Harding's manner — it was once recalled — "was still and moderate," but gradually he became more and more agitated. His mind and words began to run off in all kinds of directions, and then his voice became louder and louder and his "speech . . . rapid and indistinct . . . until at length little was heard but a sound, loud, confused and intensely earnest." Next there were "copious tears" and uncontrolled "unrestrained action and movement."[80]

For Harding the Holy Spirit was at work, and for many of those who heard him there was a powerful sense of understanding and of empathy with the preacher and the message with which they obviously resonated.

Harding was able to create an intense human involvement with the present — with here-and-now existence — as well as with the indefinite, eternal future. His words, and his tears, obviously had a great impact on his listeners. It was as though his sometimes disjointed words, permeated with intense feeling, captured the essence of the Christian gospel. For many, it was a shattering psychological experience; it was as if the entire New Testament was suddenly uttered in one prolonged Harding sentence. Being powered projections, Harding's words took upon themselves an aura of power.[81]

It was ironic and perhaps only fitting that the man who, according to his biographer, "gloried to the last"[82] that he was a "New Light," first and foremost, and who also found it so difficult to abandon his "New Dispensationalism," should witness the undermining of the "Reformation" by friends putting forward arguments he had used a decade or so earlier. There is a particularly evocative description of these enthusiasts in J. Davis's *Life and Times of the Late Rev. Harris Harding*:

> They had no regard for order or government in the church. Frills, ruffles, all adornments in dress, were their abomination; and they quarreled with Mr. Harding because he would not preach against such things. They brought their peculiarities into the Conference meetings, and warm discussions were held upon them there. They attacked their minister in public, and openly contradicted him. They ascended the pulpit — even the sisters, in the heat of their inspiration — stood at his side — and commanded him to hold his peace. The worship of God was thus changed into confusion and hubbub. Then these people would collect their finery, and commit it to the flames. Some would even take their crockery and china-ware from their shelves, and bury them. They would enter into minute confession of their sins before promiscuous assemblages. They would form processions in the night, and parade the streets, exclaiming "Behold the Bridegroom cometh! Behold the Bridegroom cometh!" Such were the demonstrations to which these people were led by the spirit that was in them, and which they fondly deemed to be the Spirit of God.[83]

Not only did Harding experience a sickening dose of his own spiritual medicine, he also in 1809 reluctantly withdrew his church from the Baptist Association. The precipitating issue was close communion. In 1808 former friends — and ex-New Dispensationalists — argued that in order to ensure continued Baptist growth, it was essential to abandon, once and for all, open communion. It was contended that "if believer's baptism is the only baptism of the New Testament, those who have been sprinkled in infancy, or afterwards, [were not] lawfully admissible to the Lord's Supper."[84]

At the 1808 Association meeting held at Cornwallis, the problem was finally resolved. Harris Harding supported open communion, maintaining that the prime concern of the Baptist ministers was to "rely entirely upon that divine influence with which the apostles were favoured when they were setting men apart for the work of the ministry, or building up the church of God," and he "entreated them not to be particular respecting external order or outward forms, which would all perish in the using." Harding was attacked by Theodore Harding, who "observed that when the tabernacle was to be erected in the wilderness divine direction was given respecting every part, even for the loops . . . He considered that the Great Head of the church should be in like manner followed with under-rating strictness."[85] This argument was enthusiastically endorsed by the Reverend Henry Hale, visiting Calvinist Baptist preacher from Massachusetts, who was eager to neutralize "New Light" zeal with Calvinist Baptist "strictness."

Eventually three churches — Yarmouth, Argyle and Chester — withdrew from the Baptist Association, and each of these churches had. close ties with Harris Harding. In 1808 there were 1,248 members in the eleven Nova Scotia churches belonging to the Association. In 1809, after the withdrawal, there were only 753 in the eight close-communion Baptist churches.[86] Harris Harding's church had been the second largest in the Association — 250-strong in comparison with Horton's 276. It was not until 1828 that Harding's church was reunited to the Association.[87] In 1811 Chester rejoined, and in 1837 Argyle, in somewhat different form, returned to the Baptist fold.[88]

When Harris Harding died in 1854, his church had over 700 members, and a decade later it was calculated that there were more than 2,000 Baptists in the Yarmouth region "under the care of *eight* pastors."[89] Harding had found it difficult to die the Christian death. He could not, observed his biographer, "taste those raptures in which he had been wont to luxuriate, regarding them as special proofs of the presence and power of the Holy Spirit."[90] All the old Christian warrior could say on his deathbed was "Good words! good words! But the Lord was not here — the Lord was not here."[91]

V

It would be a mistake to exaggerate Harding's importance in the fascinating symbiotic relationship connecting Nova Scotia's Second Great Awakening with the transformation of the New Light movement into the Calvinist Baptist Church. Nor should Harding's role be underestimated. He certainly was not a charismatic religious leader in the Alline tradition. Nor was he an organizational genius in the Timothy Dwight mould. But, it may be argued, he was — almost despite himself — an important link between the First and the Second Great Awakenings. In a very real sense he succeeded in applying the Alline paradigm of revitalization to another chronological period and to a different mix of people.[92] Harding, in many respects, was a sensitive reflector of the religious aspirations of the thousands of Nova Scotians to whom he diligently preached his highly emotional and introspective version of the Christian gospel. American influences, direct and indirect, events in Europe and economic and social stress in Nova Scotia may have provided the general framework in which the Second Great Awakening worked itself out. Yet without men like Harding, no "Great Reformation" would have been possible; and without him, moreover, the "Great Reformation" would have been quite a different kind of religious movement.[93]

Chapter V

Kingston Methodists and Baptists
and the Great Religious Revival of 1852 and 1853

I

Many English-Canadian historians seem to find it very difficult to take religion seriously. As they comb the past for relevance and what has been recently called the collective *Habits of the Heart*,[1] they are keen to avoid any confrontation with spiritual and religious realities. Perhaps they are uncomfortable thinking about such issues, which could trigger in their unconscious powerful feelings of guilt and anxiety. Perhaps, because of the older political and constitutional bias of so much Canadian historical writing and the newer bias of secular social history — now a kind of revised standard version of Canada's past — they are determined to float in the mainstream of historiography and not be lost in some shallow cul-de-sac. With understandable concern for their professional futures, they are not eager to be shoved off to what to many would be regarded as the dark periphery of their discipline.

It may also be the case that a number of English-Canadian historians avoid the serious study of the role of religion in shaping the contours of our collective past because they instinctively and perceptively realize that religion was really of little consequence. They look at the present and see an increasingly irrelevant Christian church propagating increasingly irrelevant Christian doctrine at an increasingly apathetic and secular audience. They read into the past what they perceive in the present and the result, as might be expected, is a largely secular story. If religion is considered, it is not considered in its own right but as a peripheral factor influencing, either negatively or positively, the political, social, economic and intellectual development of Canada. And for the fastest-growing group within the historical profession, the working-class historians, religion is of little consequence indeed. It is not even the "opiate of the people"; it is an inconsequential mumbo-jumbo from a more primitive age — something perhaps to be mentioned in passing as a not especially clever hoax perpetuated by some priestly charlatans. Too much of the new working-class history, in my view, is written with little or no appreciation of religious realities. It is E. P. Thompson without religion, and the end result is bound to be a serious distortion of our collective past. To argue that religion's role in Canadian "working-class life" is, as has recently been contended, "shrouded in obscurity and ambivalence"[2] and nothing else is to avoid grappling with a problem which might, in fact, shatter the prevailing working-class paradigm.

This, of course, may be regarded as an unfair caricature of the Canadian historical profession. Yet the exaggeration should nevertheless underscore some of the basic problems confronting the writing of religious history in English Canada in the 1980s. When compared, for example, with American historiography, it is clear tht English-Canadian historians throughout this century have significantly downplayed the importance of religion as a formative force in Canadian life. There is no Canadian Perry Miller; there is therefore no "Puritan Frontier" paradigm in which to carefully fit unfolding historical events. There is no Canadian William McLoughlin; there is no "Revival-Revitalization" conceptual framework in which to interpret the possible symbiotic relationship existing between religious change and profound social change. There is no George Marsden; there is therefore no overarching theme which links premillennial fundamentalism with neo-conservatism. There is no Martin Marty; there is no richly textured story of *Pilgrims in Their Own Land.* Moreover, there is no Robert Bellah; there is no civil religion thesis which tries to encompass the widespread drift to individualism, on the one hand, and the yearning for a community, on the other. Yet we do have *The Regenerators,* Ramsay Cook's attempt to understand the corrosive influence of secularism on Canadian Protestantism, or at least its Upper Canadian variant.

For me, good historical writing must always try to link effectively and sensitively the past and the present, the local and the national. Links of this kind must at least be attempted and perhaps even built. Our collective religious experience as Kingstonians — a crucially important "habit of the heart" — provides, in my view, one of these key links. We owe so much of the essential meaning of our lives to our religious traditions about which, unfortunately, we now infrequently think. And we face, I think, a very real possibility that the further undermining of these traditions "may eventually deprive us of that meaning altogether."[3] I am,

Over and over again the typical Methodist camp meeting in North America would be described as a place engulfed by "heavenly fire." "Before he had finished singing the fourth verse," a Methodist evangelist observed, "the *power of God* came down, and pervaded the vast assembly, and it became agitated — swelling and surging like the sea in a storm."[10] The camp meeting was indeed a vast, communal, spiritual, "swelling and surging... sea." In North America it had obviously "moved beyond the once-radical field preaching that Wesley and Whitefield had instituted, shifting attention from conspicuous preaching performances to congregational participation." Moreover, the Methodist preachers "made overt attempts to have the power of God 'strike fire' over a mass audience; they encouraged uncensored testimonials by persons without respect to age, sex, or race; the public sharing of private ecstasy; overt physical display and emotional release; loud and spontaneous response to preaching; and the use of folk music that would have chilled the marrow of Charles Wesley."[11]

At the level of popular evangelical religion in Upper Canada in the first half of the nineteenth century, especially at the Methodist cutting edge, was to be found a striking pattern of alternation "between opposite poles of strict self-containment and shared communal outpouring."[12] The privatization of Upper Canadian houses with what has been referred to as "increasingly individualized furnishing" and the repressive discipline and boundary creation of the new evangelical discipline underscored a move toward tighter controls and individualism. But, on the other hand, the ecstatic releases associated with revivalism "manifested a continuing need for unconstrained bodily communication." It may be argued that

> in the same way their changing material conditions of life left them torn in two directions between individualizing trends of contemporary Anglo-American culture and the appeal of the surviving communalism of their own traditions. On the one hand, a segregation of the physical self, on the other hand, a free acceptance of close bodily contact.[13]

It is noteworthy that the camp meeting continued to play a crucial role in the religious life of Upper Canadian Methodism — well into the 1850s — long after it had lost much of its appeal even in the American Midwest and South.

It is necessary in any sophisticated examination of religion as an aspect of popular culture to apply insights from the growing field of ethnography — that branch of anthropology "directed to the interpretation of particular cultures."[14] It is not enough, of course, to be slavishly dependent upon the written record. Emphasis must also be placed upon "gesture, demeanor, dress, architecture" and what has been described as "all the codes by which those who share in the culture convey meanings and significance to each other."[15] The task of the scholar is to identify and to link patterns of behavior — these "interlocking sets of paradigms or metaphors" — and transform them into "more or less coherent maps of experience."[16] Religious life should be understood as "it was experienced by 'actors' on 'past stages,' each playing his or her own part, and responding to the roles of others in ways that expressed their particular conceptions of the nature of the 'play.'"[17]

Upper Canadian and Ontario popular religion provides an excellent "past stage" and a "myriad of actors" for the enterprising and imaginative historian. For example, there is Nathan Bang's famous description of the 1805 Hay Bay Camp Meeting. It was a prolonged religious meeting attended by almost one-quarter of the entire Upper Canadian population at the time — if Bang's numbers are at all accurate. Bang's remarkable description merely underscores the importance of camp meetings in early nineteenth century Upper Canadian Methodism:

> The night was clear and serene, and the scene being new to us, a peculiar solemnity rested upon all our minds. The lights glowing among the trees and above the tents, and the voice of prayer and praise mingling and ascent into the starlight night, altogether inspired the heart with emotions better felt than described. During this meeting six persons passed from death unto life. At five o'clock Saturday morning a prayer-meeting was held, and at ten o'clock a sermon was preached on the text, "My people are destroyed for lack of knowledge." At this time the congregation had increased to perhaps twenty-five hundred, and the people of God were seated together on logs near the stand, while a crowd were standing in a semi-circle around them. During the sermon I felt an unusual sense of the Divine presence, and thought I could see a cloud of Divine glory rest upon the congregation. The circle of spectators unconsciously fell back step by step, until quite a space was opened between them and those who were seated. At length I sprang from my seat to my feet. The preacher stopped, and said, "Take it up and go on!" "No, I rise not to preach." I immediately descended from the stand among the hearers; the rest of the preachers all spontane-

ously followed me, and we went among the people, exhorting the impenitent and comforting the distressed; for while Christians were filled with "joy unspeakable and full of glory," many a sinner was praying and weeping in the surrounding crowd. These we collected in little groups, and exhorted God's people to join in prayer with them, and not to leave them till he should save their souls. O what a scene of tears and prayers was this! I suppose that not less than a dozen little praying circles were thus formed in the course of a few minutes. It was truly affecting to see parents weeping over their children, neighbors exhorting their unconverted neighbors to repent, while all, old and young, were awe-struck. The wicked looked on with silent amazement, while they beheld some of their companions struck down by the mighty power of God, and heard his people pray for them. The mingled voices of prayer and praise were heard afar off, and produced a solemn awe apparently upon all minds. Struck by the grandeur of the spectacle and the religious interests of the crowd, a preacher mounted the stand and proclaimed for his text, "Behold he cometh with clouds, and every eye shall see him." The meeting continued all night, and few, I think, slept that night. During this time some forty persons were converted or sanctified ... After breakfast, a host being on the ground, we held a love-feast. The interest and excitement were so great, and the congregation so large, that while some assembled around the stand, a preacher mounted a wagon at the distance and addressed a separate congregation. The impression of the word was universal, the power of the Spirit was manifested throughout the whole encampment, and almost every tent was a scene of prayer. At noon the Lord's Supper was administered to multitudes, while other multitudes looked on with astonishment; a young woman of fashionable and high position in society, was smitten, and with sobs entreated the prayers of the people. Her sister forced her away; a preacher went forth without the camp and led them both back, followed by quite a procession of their friends; a circle gathered around them and sang and prayed. The unawakened sister was soon upon her knees praying in agony, and was first converted; the other quickly after received the peace of God, and they wept and rejoiced together. A backslider, who had become a maniac, and was in despair, was brought to the camp. His symptoms were like those of the New Testament demoniacs. It required the strength of several men to hold him; especial prayer was offered for him. We first besought

God, for Christ's sake, to restore him his faculties, which was done. He then earnestly prayed for himself, and before the meeting closed he was not only delivered from despair, but filled with joy and peace in believing.

The time was at hand at last for the conclusion of the meeting. The last night was the most awfully impressive and yet delightful scene my eyes ever beheld. There was not a cloud in the sky. The stars studded the firmament, and the glory of God filled the camp. All the neighboring forest seemed vocal with the echos of hymns. Turn our attention which ever way we would, we heard the voice of prayer and praise. As it was the last night, every moment seemed precious; parents were praying for their children and children for their parents, brothers and sisters for one another, neighbors for neighbors, all anxious that before they left the consecrated ground they should be "sealed as the heirs of salvation." I will not attempt to describe the parting scene, for it was indescribable. The preachers, about to disperse to their distant fields of labor, hung upon each other's necks, weeping and yet rejoicing. Christians from remote settlements, who had here formed holy friendships which they expected would survive in heaven, parted probably to meet no more on earth, but in joyful hope of re-union above. They wept, prayed, sang, shouted aloud, and at last had to break away from each other as by force. As the hosts marched off in different directions the songs of victory rolled along the highways. Great was the good that followed.[18]

In January 1841, thirty-six years after the famous Hay Bay Camp Meeting, what has been called a "typical" Methodist revival was taking place in Maltilda, in the Niagara Peninsula. It was reported in the *Christian Guardian* on February 10, 1841:

This meeting is still progressing, and night after night the altar is crowded with penitents, with heart-rending sighs and tears flowing amain, declaring that they never would give up their suit until they should know that God had power on earth to save such hell-deserving sinners. O, sir, to see the chapel covered with the spiritually slain, what a blessed sight it is. Husbands and wives, parents and children, all in a kind of regular confusion, weeping, exhorting, praying and rejoicing alternately with and for each other. So graciously has God engaged in the hearts of the people, in quest of salvation, that at times I have had much to do to prevail on them to disperse and go home.

At Matilda, in 1841, the camp meeting had been brought into the Methodist chapel — at least for the winter.

According to Russel B. Nye, popular culture, broadly defined, "confirms the experience of the majority, in contrast to elite art, which tends to explore the new." Consequently, popular culture, including evangelical religion, "has been an unusually sensitive reflector" of the spiritual values of society. The articulation of evangelical religion then "corroborates ... values and attitudes already familiar to his or her audience." For the popular preacher or the lay exhorter "predictability is important" as well as the underscoring of "the fulfillment of expectation, the pleasant shock of recognition of the known" and the "verification of an experience already familiar."[19] There is the tendency, then, in religious revivals to try to return to the pristine purity of a New Testament past — a past which both soothes and convicts. As José Ortega had suggested, "For the very reason that to live is to feel oneself propelled toward the future, we recoil from it as from a greased slide and fall back into the past, towards the future, our future which we must bring into being."[20]

III

James Caughey, the great nineteenth-century Methodist evangelist, was the catalyst for the Great Kingston Revival of 1852 and 1853, and he helped many Upper Canadians to "fall back into the past, toward the future." Born in Ireland in 1810, Caughey, when still a teenager, immigrated to New York with his parents. He died in Vermont in 1891. Rejecting the Calvinist heritage of his parents, Caughey was converted in 1830 in Troy, New York, during a revival meeting in a Methodist Episcopal church. The following year, the twenty-one-year-old Caughey, who worked in a local flour mill, was accepted as a probationary lay preacher by the Troy Conference of the Methodist Episcopal Church.[21]

A close friend and associate, the Reverend Daniel Wiseman, once described Caughey in this way:

Mr. Caughey was a self-educated man. He has been an extensive reader, and his mind is richly stored with the best thoughts of the best English writers. He possesses a remarkably vivid imagination, which in its ardent flights, sometimes, though not often, soars into the suburbs of fanciful regions ... Nature formed him a man above the mediocrity of men, but she did not endow him with the highest gifts of genius. The church has many ministers of larger powers, more highly cultivated, better read, and of higher intellectual rank, but whose success in God's work will not bear comparison with those of Mr. Caughey.[22]

In 1835 Caughey, who was then located in Vermont, made his first evangelistic foray into what is now Canada. He conducted a series of revival meetings in Montreal. A contemporary described Caughey's spiritual impact on Montreal in the following manner:

> This man of God seems eminently qualified to lead forward the Israel of God to the promised rest of perfect love, and we rejoice that God has graciously prepared the hearts of his people in this place, for His holy and evangelical message to them. The afternoons have been devoted to this special object, and Mr. Caughey had delivered a number of discourses on this most important subject such as will be remembered through time and eternity by those who had the privilege of hearing them.[23]

The "special object" of Caughey's preaching referred to was his emphasis on holiness and the second blessing of sanctification.

During the 1840s Caughey conducted a series of revival meetings in Lower Canada, New Brunswick, Great Britain and the United States. During the time he was in Britain, from 1841 to 1847, it was claimed that Caughey was responsible for 20,000 conversions and 9,000 separate experiences of "entire sanctification."[24] It is noteworthy that Caughey's message — a blend of the old Wesleyan Methodism of the eighteenth century and the dynamic preaching style of the Second Great Awakening — had a profound impact on William Booth, the founder of the Salvation Army. Furthermore, the message and its impact established Caughey's reputation as one of the most influential American evangelists in nineteenth-century Britain.

Caughey returned to British North America in November 1851, when he helped to coax into existence major revivals in Toronto and Kingston. Kingston Methodists, as early as 1850, had wanted to invite Caughey to their city but did not formally do so until the completion of the imposing Sydenham Street Wesleyan Church in the spring of 1852. They felt that they did not have an edifice large enough to house the presence of the great American evangelist. Caughey arrived in Kingston late in

November 1852, and the revival-holiness meetings immediately began.

In 1851 the population of Kingston, according to the census of that year, was 11,585. Ten years later the population had grown to 13,743. In 1851, according to the census, there were 1,175 Wesleyan Methodists — adherents and not members — and in 1861, 1,550. In 1851 there were only 135 Baptists; ten years later there were 174. On the other hand, in 1851, 4,110 Kingstonians were Anglicans and 3,712, Roman Catholics. Ten years later there were 4,129 Anglicans and 4,638 Roman Catholics. Thus, the latter two denominations combined, in 1851, to make up close to seventy percent of the total Kingston population while the Wesleyan Methodists constituted some ten percent and the Baptists only a little more than one percent.[25]

Caughey preached at least ten times a week in Kingston and, according to contemporaries, with "great power." "His preaching," it was noted, "is terribly searching" and the so-called sandy foundations "of doubt were shaken to their depths." As far as the local Methodist leader Samuel Rice was concerned, from his vantage point early in 1853:

> The character of the work has been rather peculiar — quiet and steady, but constantly progressing. At first, those who were desirous of "pleasing God in all things" [and] felt the necessity of a clean heart came forward in large numbers, seeking full salvation; and a goodly number entered into that liberty. The convictions have been deep, and the conversions clear. The persons who have been the subject of the work are mostly adults. I have before my mind at the present, nearly a score of husbands, who in the company with their wives, have been made partakers of the precious faith of the Gospel ... The work has not been confined to those who were hearers in our church; but the members of other churches have doubtless found mercy.[26]

Even though he was not particularly sympathetic to religious revivals, the editor of the Kingston *Daily British Whig* felt compelled on March 11, 1853, to observe:

> Although Mr. Caughey can make no claim to deep learning, nor even brilliant eloquence, there is an original turn of thought and a striking expression which never fails to command attention, and seldom allows his hearers to depart without something to meditate upon. This is the grand secret of preaching which drew multitudes to hear the fathers of the Protestant church John Knox, Calvin and

others. While they spoke to the head, they appealed to the heart with
an enthusiasm which carried conviction with it.

One of Caughey's Toronto converts, W. H. Pearson, once described
Caughey in the following manner:

> Mr. Caughey's appearance as he entered the pulpit always impressed
> me. It seemed as if he had come from the very presence of God, so
> radiant was his face. He always prayed like one who had direct access
> to the throne of grace, and sometimes a wonderful influence rested
> on the people while he supplicated God on their behalf. He was not
> what might be called a handsome man, he was dark complexioned,
> his features regular and his face indicated a great strength of charac-
> ter, and when in repose was rather stern. His voice was not exactly
> musical but not plain and of great compass and his enunciation very
> distinct, so that even when he lowered his voice to almost a whisper
> he could be heard throughout the whole church.

Pearson then went on: "His sermons [were] generally colloquial and
abounded with apt illustrations from many sources. He spoke with such a
kind persuasiveness, when pleading with sinners that it seemed to melt
every heart, but at times his denunciations of sin were terrific as he painted
the awful doom that awaited the inpenitent."[27]

One of the major reasons for Caughey's success in Kingston was his
remarkable ability to help Kingstonians, in a profound sense, "to fall back
into the past, towards the future," as Ortega had put it. It has been recently
argued that

> Caughey ... became a bridge for a large number of people in Upper
> Canadian society in the 1850s. For recent arrivals [from Britain] he
> was a bridge to the homeland. For Canadian Methodists he was a
> bridge between the old revivalistic style of an earlier day and the
> respectability of the present. He provided a way for his hearers to
> have their feet in a past experience, while reaching ahead to the new
> realities of a more and more urban society. Like all successful
> evangelists then, he met the people where they were and took them
> with him to where he was going. Caughey's revivalistic style itself
> shows this balancing between the old and the new. In many ways he
> symbolized the new revivalism that was to characterize American
> religious life at the end of the century. Caughey — like D. L. Moody

after him — used the city for his meeting place and consciously marshalled the church around him to help spread the revival; this and his interdenominational outlook were forerunners of a later revival style. But his rhetoric, preaching styles and message looked back to an older time. In this way he struck a responsive chord among Canadian Wesleyan Methodists, who were caught between the habits of the past and a recognition of the need to be part of the rapidly changing world.[28]

Caughey preached his last sermon in Sydenham Street Methodist Church on March 13, 1853. During his less than four-month sojourn in Kingston, Caughey, it was asserted, had been directly responsible for close to 400 conversions or experiences of sanctification. It is noteworthy that in June 1852 the Kingston Methodist circuit reported 363 members; in June 1853 it reported 475. There was, of course, significant growth in Methodist churches surrounding Kingston. Hundreds of Methodists and others from the Kingston hinterland had flocked to the Sydenham Street Methodist Church to hear Caughey. The Wesleyan Methodists in the Napanee region added close to 100 new members during the June 1852 and June 1853 period, while those in Newburgh added seventy-seven and Wilton, forty.[29]

Kingston area Methodists were not the only group significantly affected by Caughey's evangelistic campaign, however; so too were Kingston Baptists. Kingston Presbyterians and Anglicans and Congregationalists, however, showed little interest in Caughey, and their church records as well as their lack of numerical growth in the 1852–53 period clearly underscored this fact.[30]

According to the leader of the Sydenham Street Methodist Church, Caughey's "indefatigable and evangelical labour" had been responsible for "the present vigorousness and devotedness of the Wesleyan Church in this City."[31] The revival he helped bring into existence had quite a different impact on Kingston Baptists. At first the revival resulted in an unprecedented number of adult baptisms in the First Baptist Church. For example, in 1852 there was only one baptism in First Baptist; in March 1853 there were 32, and in April, 30. But by the late summer of 1853, the church was badly split, largely because of the revival and the divisiveness unleased by the charismatic disciple of Caughey, the Reverend J. F. Bishop.[32]

IV

Much less is known about Bishop than about Caughey, and far less
is known about the Kingston Baptists than about the Kingston Methodists. On July 9, 1840, four Kingston men and seven women, together with
the Reverend J. Dyer, recently arrived from England, "were constituted"
as the First Baptist Church, Kingston. Within two years the Baptists had
their own brick building on Johnson Street (now the Greek Orthodox
Church). There were two important Baptist founding families — the
Haineses and the Anguses — and the real leader of the congregation, until
his untimely death on September 25, 1841, was G. H. Haines. Without the
leadership of Haines — a man whose "religious views were comprehensi-
ble and liberal"[33] — the church was dissolved in January 1844 and not
reconstituted until December 15, 1844. Thus, a strict reading of the formative period of First Baptist Church would locate the actual origins of the
present church in December 1844 and not in the summer of 1840.

The decade preceding the arrival of Reverend Bishop witnessed the
slow growth of the congregation as well as growing tensions. There was an
open split in the congregation, for example, over the question of whether
the choir leader should or should not be a duly converted Christian. There
was a minor disruption over the introduction of an organ; moreover, there
was considerable tension between the old-English founders of the church
and the newly arrived Scots Baptists, one of whom was Alexander Mac-
kenzie, second prime minister of Canada, and also between these two
groups and a small but vociferous American group of Baptists. There was
also some friction between open- and close-communion advocates, as
well as between Free Will and Calvinist Baptists.

The first minister of the reconstituted First Baptist Church was the
Reverend Alexander Lorimer, who formally accepted a call to the church
on January 15, 1845. Lorimer had been the minister of Helen Street
Baptist Church in Montreal before coming to Kingston, and his former
church "state[d] their entyre approbation and warmly recomend[ed]"
him.[34] Lorimer was not a very dynamic minister; he seemed to devote most
of his time and energy in keeping his fragile church together. There was a
core of thirty or so active members during most of his ministry, which
ended in November 1852, but he brought few new converts into the
church. He baptized only one person in 1845, two in 1846, one in 1847,
none in 1848, one in 1849, five in 1850, two in 1851 and one in 1852. A
special church meeting held on February 23, 1848, indicated that the
church desperately wanted a revival but felt that Lorimer was not the

person to bring one about. "The object of the meeting" was to "consider the propriety of holding a series of meetings for the revival of the Lord's work amongst us." The church members

> one after another expressed that it would be desirable such an effort be made upon which the church resolved that a series of meetings be held. Resolved also that the Pastor write to Bro. McPhail of Osgood [near Ottawa] to request him to come and aid us in this special effort. The propriety of making the matter a subject of prayer, & of holding some preparatory meeting to the ones contemplated being suggested, the meeting was closed.

However, the Reverend McPhail, a noted Baptist evangelist, refused to come, and the church decided in late March 1848 to have its own revival meetings. These were, the evidence suggests, embarrassingly unsuccessful.

Sensitive to growing criticism in his church, Lorimer, on September 3, 1852, first indicated that he was considering "the duty of resigning the office [of pastor] into the hands of the Church." Then, on September 10, 1852, a letter from Reverend Lorimer was read to a special church meeting:

> Dear Brethren,
> After many conflicts of mind and some uncertainty as to what is the path of duty, I resign into your hands the Office of Pastor over you. It is becoming that I state to you the reasons that have prompted me to take this step.
> It is not because of want of affection toward the church. Since I became your Pastor (now nearly eight years old) I do not know that I ever felt the church to be dearer to me than it is at present. The continued proof of your affection toward me and mine; the favour with which you have received my unworthy ministrations in the word of truth, and the unremitted exertions you have made, in the face of many discouraging circumstances, to sustain the institutions of the gospel — have justly endeared you to my heart.
> Nor is it because of any less interest in those distinctive truths which characterise us as a body of Christians in this city. The importance of holding forth these distinctive truths both in word and deed, deepens rather than abates, the longer I meditate on them.
> Nor is it because of any prospect of entering into any other pastoral relation. If this step is of the Lord, he can direct and

provide; but it is not taken with any new relation sought or in view.

When I first thought of placing back in your hands the office of Pastor, one reason among others was a lack of vigour of mind arising perhaps from a little bodily indisposition. This reason is partially removed, although now I feel I could not devote that vigour of mind to the work of the ministry which is here needed and which its importance demands.

I hope that a change of pastors may be blessed of God, to the enlargement of the church and to the development and increase of holiness in *all* the members composing it, is the main reason for the step I now take. I hope that by a change it may please God to remove the spiritual insensibility which now so greatly prevails among the unconverted, induce many to attend who now do not — and so carry home the truth to all that the preaching of the word and the institutions of the gospel may not — by any cause — be rendered powerless. From causes apparent — such as the increase of new congregations above the increase of the inhabitants, and the consequent drawing off of hearers to these, as the removal of individuals to other parts of the land, as the disaffection caused by the exhibition of the truth which cuts *to* the heart but does not subdue it, and thus proving a savour of death unto death prompts men to avoid it, — or from causes deeper and less obvious than these — the number of hearers is few; while on the other hand in looking over the city, it would seem as if God had a great work for his people here to do, and an important mission for them to fulfill.

In the present state of the church and congregation, I place in your hands the office to which you have called me because that though out of regard to my feelings you might be loath to mention it, yet I would not wish to burden the church with a heavier load, in the way of support that they might feel able to bear. To continue to raise what you have done may be a greater effort than you feel you can perform; and I do not wish to suffer the church to be put in an embarrassed condition when perhaps by a change this might be avoided.

Then Lorimer concluded his fascinating letter:

And, now, dear Brethren, assuring you of the affection I bear you and of the deep interest I feel and hope ever to cherish in your spiritual well being and in the cause of our common Saviour in

Kingston, and hoping you may be divinely guided in the choice of a successor in office, I remain.

Your brother in Christ,
Alexander Lorimer

Kingston, Sept. 10, 1852.

The Lorimer letter was fascinating not only for what it actually said but also for what it seemed to imply. What Lorimer appeared to be telling the church was that his past "bodily indisposition" as well as the spiritual lassitude of his congregation were together responsible for the lack of any real growth, in terms of members and "holiness," in First Baptist Church, Kingston. He was also, it is clear, asking the church to endorse his ministry and perhaps pay what it owed him. It was a tactful way of saying, If you want me to continue, show your support in a tangible manner, not necessarily by providing me with a raise, but with the funds you have not paid me from previous years.

On September 14 the church promised "with as little delay as possible to make up the present deficiency." In addition, Lorimer was "affectionately" requested to "alter his mind with regard to resigning his charge of this church at the present time." The following day Lorimer "stated to the church that having considered the purport of the resolution sent to him he deemed it an indication of Providence that he should withdraw his resignation & at present remain as Pastor of the church in accordance with their desire."

Not everyone in the church, however, was pleased with Lorimer's decision. Sensing a growing opposition, Lorimer, after the evening service on Sunday, November 14, 1852, announced from the pulpit "that this would be probably the last time he would have an opportunity of addressing his brethren." He would have "been happy" to have remained as pastor "had all the church united in labouring to extend the cause of our common Lord, but as some had seen fit not to do he thought it would be folly to continue."

There is no explicit evidence to suggest how large the anti-Lorimer faction actually was in the church. It is clear, however, that a vociferous minority was opposed, and there is some circumstantial evidence to suggest that D. D. Calvin may have been a ringleader in the anti-Lorimer group. Calvin was a remarkable man: a successful entrepreneur, a gifted Conservative politician, the "king" of Garden Island and, toward the end of his life, a key member of the First Baptist Church, Kingston.

Calvin was born in Vermont in May 1798. He moved with his family to northern New York and eventually established himself after 1835 as a timber entrepreneur in the Clayton region. Because he saw greater economic opportunities in the Kingston area, Calvin moved permanently to the eastern end of Garden Island sometime in 1844. When he died on May 18, 1884, on Garden Island, he left an estate conservatively valued at $324,000. His biographer has referred to Calvin as "one of the eccentrics of the early days of Ontario." For example, he was always suspicious of men who bit their fingernails, he detested short men and he had "an abiding contempt for dogs and their owners."[35]

Professor Donald Swainson has pointed out that Calvin was converted during the winter of 1842–43, when a religious revival swept Clayton, "led by the Baptist and Methodist Episcopal Churches." Calvin, however, was not baptized by immersion until after his non-Baptist wife died on July 4, 1843. "For the remainder of his life," according to Professor Swainson, "Calvin was a devout and active member of the Baptist church."[36] Calvin may have been a devout Baptist, but he certainly was not an active member of the First Baptist Church, Kingston, until after Lorimer's resignation in November 1852. In other words, from 1844, when he settled permanently on Garden Island, until December 1852, Calvin's name is never even mentioned in the records of the First Baptist Church.

Why did Calvin not join the First Baptist Church soon after 1844? Perhaps he disliked Lorimer — who may have chewed his fingernails or else was a short gentleman who loved dogs. Or it may have been that Calvin, a Yankee Baptist converted in the Burned-Over District of New York state, felt very much ill at ease in the rather staid, conservative and lifeless British Kingston Baptist Church.

What Lorimer may have been alluding to in his letter of resignation and in his statement to the church was that wealthy people like Calvin were not eager to support his ministry. In the final analysis, as the Christian ministry moved towards professionalization and respectability, those who controlled the purse strings of the church increasingly controlled the style and substance of the message being preached.

The first reference made to D. D. Calvin in the First Baptist Church records is to be found in a brief description of a "Special Meeting of the Church and Society of the Baptist Church" held on December 21, 1852. It was "unanimously resolved that an invitation be given to the Revd J. F. Bishop to become their Pastor." It was also decided that

the following Brethren and Friends be appointed a Committee of
arrangements, & extend the call and make arrangements with our
Pastor elect for his settlement and support: —

Viz: D. D. Calvin Esq.
      M. L. Green
      Dr. Sutton
      J. F. Skinner
      Wm. Holgate
      S. P. White

Calvin and Sutton, it should be pointed out, were not even members of the
church. In fact, Sutton never became a member — his wife did — and
Calvin became a member "By Experience & Letter" on March 4, 1853.

V

The contemporaneous arrival of D. D. Calvin and the Reverend J.
F. Bishop at the Kingston Baptist Church in December 1852 was
obviously no accident. Both men had resided in Jefferson County in upper
New York state, and there is every indication that they were friends there.
Moreover, Bishop may have been directly responsible for Calvin's conversion in 1842–43. What is definitely known is that Bishop preached his first
sermon at First Baptist in the evening service on December 12. He
preached in the morning and evening on December 19, and then two days
later, at a "special meeting of the Church and Society of the Baptist
Church," it was unanimously resolved to invite Bishop to be "their
Pastor."

On December 27 Bishop gave his considered reply to the Kingston
Baptist "call." He seemed to be particularly concerned about the terms of
his employment, demanding, among other things, that he should be given
"three months notice" before being asked to leave the church and that he
be permitted to use "the Vestery of the Church for School purposes." He
was to be paid a yearly salary of £600 "to be raised from said resources
over and above the use of the Parsonage & Vestery as aforesaid." In
addition, "the Church and Congregation" were to be "annually invited to
pay a pastoral donation visit" in order to supplement his yearly salary.
And, finally, since Bishop was in great demand as a visiting evangelist, he
was to "have the privilege of relaxation from his duties some ten or twelve
sabbaths in the year."

Bishop had bargained from strength. He knew he had Calvin's support and he also realized that the Kingston Baptists were desperately concerned about reviving their church before it died a slow and inglorious death, so Bishop was not surprised that on December 27 the Kingston Baptists "considered and unanimously accepted" his "proposals." He immediately began to spread the Caughey revival from the neighboring Sydenham Street Methodist Church, down Johnson Street, to the First Baptist Church. Bishop and Calvin had worked closely with Methodists in northern New York during revivals there. They were eager to be associated with Caughey, but they did not want all the new Kingston converts to become Methodists. They therefore began a series of special revival meetings in the First Baptist Church. Within a seven-month period Bishop baptized no fewer than seventy-five men and women — over three times as many people as had been baptized by his three predecessors over a thirteen-year period. In addition, seven became members "by Experience" and six by "letter of transfer" during the late December 1852-to-late July 1853 period. In August and September three other Kingstonians became members of the First Baptist Church by "letter of transfer." Thus, during his winter-spring-summer ministry in Kingston, Bishop had drawn ninety-one new members into the church, almost tripling the church's membership — but not for long. In 1851 there had been thirty-five active church members; a decade later, despite the revival, there were only forty-five.

In early February 1853 Bishop's plea for "the revival of religion in our midst" was being enthusiastically implemented. During the evening service on March 4, 1853, when D. D. Calvin finally was "received into the Church," it was observed that "at the close of the Service two young men appeared to be under conviction of sin and cried out: God be mercyful to me a Sinner." Then the "brethren and Sisters remained around the Shrine of the Cross and prayed for this conversion." The church clerk, S. P. White, concluded his brief description of the service in this manner: "Meeting dismissed at 10 O'Clock. P.M. it was alltogether a very delight-ful season — to God be all the glory."

Throughout March, daily revival meetings were held in the First Baptist Church. Young men, in particular, greatly influenced by Bishop's dynamic personality, were affected by what was frequently referred to as "the revival." Men and women at the end of revival services would emotionally "relate their Christian experiences" and beg the Almighty to accept them as redeemed sinners. For example, on Tuesday evening, March 15th, at the enquiry meeting another young person formerly a member of the Bible class, together with some men desired the prayers of God's people. Susan Gridiford told how she had found the Saviour and was desirous of following him in the ordnance of Baptism, and uniting with the Church, also Robert Webster related his experience, he having been under conviction for some time past and Bro. Holgate testifying his belief in his sincerity requested Baptism and Christian fellowship, it was resolved by the Church they be accepted.

On April 3, 1853, nineteen men and nine women became members of the church — the largest number ever given "the right hand of fellowship" at one service at the First Baptist Church. Caughey had left Kingston soon after March 13, 1853, and the centre of the revival seemed to shift, for a time, to the Baptist church. In April the church was often "filled to overflowing" as Bishop preached his revivalistic message to what the Baptist records referred to as "sinners and Christians alike." On May 15, 1853, eleven women and twelve men were admitted to membership as were Bishop and his wife Allina.

It seems that by the middle of May 1853 the revival fire was almost burned out in Kingston. Realizing this fact, Bishop and Calvin resolved to consolidate their power and influence over the Kingston congregation. On June 3, 1853, Bishop decided that D. D. Calvin, Wm. Holgate senior and S. P. White should "serve the Church as Deacons." An amendment was immediately put forward from the floor adding three names to the list — G. Davis, F. Holt and W. Skinner. Since only three deacons were to serve, a vote was "taken by ballot." There were fifty-four church members voting, and Bishop expected that his slate consisting of two older members of the church and Calvin would easily win. When the votes were counted, White received 45, Holgate 42, Holt and Davis 23 each, and Calvin and Skinner 16. Eventually Davis, who had been baptized by Bishop in March 1853, was chosen to join Holgate and White as deacon. The vote had been a devastating blow to D. D. Calvin Esq., who was obviously disliked and distrusted by a strong majority in the church. It is clear that the vote was also a sharp reprimand aimed at Bishop.

During the first week of September a deep fissure appeared in the Baptist church. One group wanted to give Bishop notice that as of December 31 his ministerial services were no longer wanted at First Baptist. Another group was determined to keep Bishop at First Baptist. At a church meeting, on September 15 it was resolved that the Meeting do now adjourn till tomorrow Evening, when the church will be called upon to give their expression, in regard to the subject brought before them this Evening, in connection with the Pastor of the Church — the subject being whether it is desirable that he remain longer than the present Year.

The September 16 church meeting was one of the most, if not the most, divisive and emotionally charged meetings in the history of First Baptist Church. It was first moved that Bishop be asked to leave the room. He adamantly "objected to this proceeding" and the motion was therefore withdrawn. Next, it was moved that Bishop be given "three months notice to leave the Church." Twenty-seven members, including Bishop and his wife, voted "Nay" and twenty-six voted "Yea." D. D. Calvin entered the fray by declaring that the anti-Bishop move was "nothing but a *drumed up* affair," and Bishop maintained that if the Meeting had agreed to his dismissal, "*he* should declare the Meeting to be nul and Void." There was yet another vote taken, and before the ballots were counted, Bishop stressed that he would now "release the Church from their former engagement, in regard to giving him a salary of £600 a year." The church clerk then reported:

> The Motion being put to the Vote amidst much confusion, the Pastor endeavouring to influence the meeting to vote for him, it was ... understood by most present that the Vote taken was in his favour, and so declared to be ...

On September 21, 1853, at yet another church meeting, it was resolved that the motion passed at the September 16 meeting was "nul and void." A special church meeting was held on September 24, attended by fifty-four church members and six adherents. It was unanimously agreed that

> believing that the interests of the Baptist Church, its peace, harmony, unity, purity, and spiritual prosperity, will be promoted, and its present unhappy and distracted state restored to its primitive tranquility and happiness, may be accomplished by the resignation of the Pastoral Office by the Revd. J. F. Bishop, we therefore most respectfully and after due consideration request the Revd. J. F. Bishop to tender his resignation of the Pastoral office.

D. D. Calvin did not attend this meeting, nor did Bishop.

Bishop's counteroffensive began on September 27, when he wrote a stinging reply to the motion passed on September 24. According to Bishop, those who had passed the motion calling for his resignation on December 31, 1853, were, in fact, "the seceding party," and he and his supporters were the "true church." Bishop concluded his letter:

> I also for myself and for the church and congregation of my charge, and for the majority of the officers therein do hereby enter this protest and extend it to all subsequent acts of similar character with the notice and resolution signed by you, and shall hold individuals responsible in every due sense for the wrongful acts with regard to said matter and for any injury that may result therefrom.

On September 27 the church met to consider the Bishop letter, and in their response the members present for the first time explicitly discussed their criticisms of Bishop. They denounced their pastor for devoting too much of his time and his energy to his private school and for "neglecting to take the advice of the officers and elder brethren." Moreover, he was condemned for his public attacks on some of his critics and for "falsly saying that Bro Calvin ordered him to lock the doors of the Chapel and Keep the Keys" and "for locking the Church doors against the rightful members thereof, those who contributed to purchase the grounds and erect the buildings long before Mr. Bishop was known to this church and, he being a comparative stranger and he never having contributed for the object." Bishop had not only refused to "pray for his enemies (or those who voted against him called so by him)," but he had also "tried to divide the Church by saying to young converts that he must get rid of those old members before he can have peace in the Church."

Bishop made things even worse when on Sunday, October 2, after unlocking the church doors, he refused communion to Deacon White. On October 5 an angry church unanimously agreed that Bishop "be notified that the doors of this church will be locked against" him, and "he is hereby forbidden to use either the Chapel or Vestery for religious purposes." In order to carry out this policy, "a Committee of 21 Male Members" was appointed to "carry out the Spirit of this Resolution." In addition, the two Kingston newspapers, *The British Whig* and the *Daily News* were to carry the following advertisement:

Notice

The Revd. J. F. Bishop is no longer Pastor of the Baptist Church, Kingston. Notice is hereby given that no public Services will be held in the Baptist Church Kingston until further notice.

By Order of the Church

S. P. White

Church Clerk

The church doors were opened on Sunday, October 23, 1853, with the Reverend Alexander Dick of Toronto preaching. Other visiting Baptist ministers preached in November and December. On January 6, 1854, the church issued a call to the Reverend Dick, a Free Will Baptist minister originally from Wyoming County, New York. Bishop had left the parsonage of the church and had by the middle of January received all the money that he was owed by the church.

After much discussion and delicate negotiations most of the pro-Bishop group returned to First Baptist Church, but not until they had helped to ease the Reverend Dick out of the pastorate by the end of March 1854. They had made it quite clear, under Calvin's leadership, that they would not support financially the Reverend Dick. They had won a battle but had lost the war, and in the process they had significantly weakened the Kingston Baptist Church at the moment it seemed to have reached the point of take-off.

The Caughey-Bishop revival, from the vantage point of March or April 1853, could be perceived as a remarkable outpouring of the Spirit of God on Kingston. From the vantage point of September or October, however, the revival had created more problems than it had resolved. Rather than bringing Baptists together, for example, it resulted in a major schism which badly split the Kingston church. And it may be argued that it took the Kingston Baptists three or four decades to recover from the Bishop controversy. For the Kingston Methodists, the Caughey revival did not bring about conflict and division, but the numbers added to the Methodist churches by Caughey in 1853 had all but disappeared by late 1854. In fact, according to P. G. Bush, "Wesleyan Methodist membership in Kingston fell rapidly after Caughey's departure to 384 in 1854 and 306 in 1855, a figure well below the peak of 475 in June 1853."[37] The revival had indeed been, it may be argued, a temporary emotional outburst largely negative in its immediate and long-term impact on the spiritual life of Kingston. On the other hand, it may also be argued that, despite some of these problems, the revival was the means whereby hundreds of Kingston and Kingston-area residents experienced the intensely satisfying and intensely pleasurable feeling of Christian fellowship as the "ecstasy of spontaneous communitas" virtually overwhelmed them. Almost despite themselves, these people, profoundly affected by the Caughey-Bishop message, were drawn by the "mystery of intimacy" toward one another.[38] For a brief time they saw Christ in their friends and their neighbors, and they wanted desperately to love their friends as they seemed to love Christ. Some Kingstonians obviously did, for a moment, and their joy must have been intense and powerful — however temporary.

Chapter VI

J. J. Sidey and the Soul Winner's Revival of the 1920s

I

One of the most interesting twentieth-century Nova Scotia evangelists was the Reverend John James Sidey.[1] Though Sidey is perhaps better known today as "the pioneer separationist of the Maritimes"[2] because of his T. T. Shields-like attempt in the 1930s to split the Maritime United Baptist Convention, he was also a very successful evangelist in the Maritimes, especially in the 1920s. His revivalistic techniques were, in a sense, nineteenth-century ones, and this helps to explain why his appeal was largely restricted to the residents of isolated and rural communities of the region. It may be argued that the religious revival he helped to bring into existence in the 1920s along the eastern shore of Nova Scotia was the last extensive revival to affect a large region of the province. The Sidey revival, therefore, may in part be viewed as a nineteenth-century social movement occurring in the twentieth century among people who felt far more at home in the previous century.

John James Sidey was born in Portsmouth, England, on December 28, 1891. His father, the Reverend Charles J. Sidey, was a Wesleyan Methodist missionary-minister in Newfoundland, where the young John spent some of his early years.[3] After this sojourn in Newfoundland, Sidey and his mother returned to England. Sidey's mother, Sarah, was a pious Methodist, but her marriage was not a happy one, and she separated permanently from her husband when she set sail from Newfoundland for Portsmouth. Consequently, it would be his mother, not his father, who would significantly influence Sidey's spiritual and emotional life at its formative stage.

At the age of fourteen John Sidey was converted, and he soon became an active member of the Pembrook Road Methodist Church, serving as a lay preacher. Encouraged by his mother, Sidey became a dentist's apprentice in Portsmouth, but because of financial problems and the fact that he had injured his right hand, he decided to emulate his father and become a Methodist missionary to the New World. However, when he left Portsmouth for Nova Scotia in the early summer of 1914, Sidey was still uncertain about his future. He was not ordained; he was not an official recruit of a Methodist Missionary Society; he was not responding to a specific call from a Nova Scotia Methodist church. He was responding to what he felt was the clear call of God to serve the cause of Jesus Christ in Nova Scotia. In his unpublished autobiography, "The Widows' Mites," written in 1961, Sidey described his "call" to full-time Christian service in the following manner:

One night I went to my room not stirring from my knees for several hours. The battle was severe. I was faced with surrender or defeat. I knew I could not go forward with my decision to work for God until the matter was settled. I remember throwing myself on the floor and crying out, "Lord Jesus I can no longer hold out against Thee, take me and cleanse me and make me everything Thou wouldst have me be." Immediately peace came into my spirit; the storm quieted and I knew God would from henceforth control my life for Himself.

Then, "a day or two" after this "surrender" experience, as Sidey described it,

[I] knelt by my chair and taking my Bible, let it fall open as the Spirit of God might direct. With closed eyes I asked the Holy Spirit to guide my hand to a verse of scripture which would be my life's promise ... Opening my eyes I noted that my right index finger was squarely over Psalm 37:5, 6 ... "Commit thy way unto the Lord, trust also in him; and He shall bring it to pass. And he shall bring forth thy righteousness as the light and thy judgment as the noonday."[4]

In 1914 Sidey saw God's finger pointing westward — toward Nova Scotia.

Soon after arriving in Halifax, Sidey made his way to his uncle, the Reverend James Heil, a Methodist minister then living in Windsor, Nova Scotia. It is clear that in the summer of 1914, despite what he might write in the 1940s and 1950s or 1960s, Sidey was disoriented and, as one of his most ardent followers has put it, "uncertain of many things."[5]

Assisting his uncle obviously did not satisfy the young Sidey, who in 1916, two years after arriving in Nova Scotia, resolved to move to the United States to benefit from "the higher training of the American universities."[6] What essentially was at the core of this decision to leave for the United States?

It has been argued that Sidey went to the United States because he had discovered that "the Nova Scotia institutions were becoming infiltrated" with "a humanistic higher criticism."[7] From his Methodist vantage point in Windsor he felt little desire, therefore, to study at Dalhousie, Acadia or even Mount Allison in New Brunswick. Instead, he thought it would be a lot safer for him, in a deep, religious sense, to enrol in two Methodist Episcopal institutions in the Chicago area — Northwestern University and Garrett Biblical Institute. Sidey endured what he once described as "one year probationary work"[8] at these two institutions within the area of the Rock River Methodist Episcopal Conference.

There might have been other reasons for Sidey's decision in 1916 to immigrate to Illinois. He may have been looking for new worlds to conquer — for a greater challenge than that provided by the relative backwater of Windsor. Or it may have been that the young Methodist left Nova Scotia because he did not want to fight for the British cause in Europe. Conscription would not come to Canada until 1917, but Sidey must have felt intense community pressure, especially in 1915 and 1916, to join in the Christian crusade to eradicate, once and for all, the Germanic anti-Christ. It may have also been the case that Sidey, who was always more positively inclined to maternal influence than fatherly-like pressure, wanted to be independent of his uncle and therefore saw in his move to Chicago a heaven-sent opportunity to resolve a number of difficult personal and career problems.

Associated with the Rock River Methodist Episcopal Conference while attending Northwestern and Garrett, Sidey supported himself financially by accepting what was called "a student pastorship." He first served three Methodist congregations located in South Chicago, Calumet Heights and Langley Avenue. A year at Northwestern and Garrett with their "modernistic teaching"[9] was more than enough for Sidey, who in 1917 transferred to Union Theological College — also located in Chicago. While studying at Union and serving as a student pastor in southern Chicago, Sidey also found time "to take up Y.M.C.A. work."[10] Near the end of the war Sidey, it has been observed, "became a visiting clergyman and clerk to the Senior Chaplain at Fort Sheridan."[11] This was part of his

Methodist pastoral work. While serving the Rock River Methodist Episcopal Conference, the Y.M.C.A. and the American army and while studying at Union Theological College, Sidey decided to work for a doctor of divinity degree at the Oriental University in Washington, D.C. After a "seven or eight months" association with Oriental University — only via correspondence, however — Sidey was awarded the D.D. degree for a short thesis entitled "Immortality, the Inevitable Result of Progressive Universe."[12] A short time after Sidey received his D.D. in 1921, Oriental University was declared a fraudulent degree-mill, and by court order its doors were permanently closed, or, more accurately, its mailbox permanently sealed. In 1921, at the same time he became a doctor of divinity (Oriental University), Sidey received the bachelor of theology degree from Union and was ordained a Methodist Episcopal minister.[13]

Three years earlier, in 1918, Sidey had returned to Nova Scotia, where he had married Edna Card, a teacher then residing in Hants County. The young couple returned to Chicago, where both of them had a great deal of difficulty dealing with urban life and the "modernism" that seemed to be bombarding the Methodist Church in the immediate postwar period. Though apparently successful at Fort Sheridan, Sidey was experiencing the deep despair of doubt, and morbid introspection seemed to immobilize him. Finally, after much spiritual turmoil, and greatly influenced by two female Salvation Army officers, Sidey found peace of mind as he jettisoned what he was learning in the classroom and replaced it with a renewed personal relationship with Christ. "It was a terrific battle," he once observed, "to rid myself of the new ideas that had been, by study and by teaching, superimposed upon the experience of my youth."[14]

While still associated with Fort Sheridan, and spurred by a new sense of evangelical zeal, Sidey and his wife became active in "the Soul Winner's Association," which had its headquarters in the St. Paul Methodist Episcopal Church, Chicago. Using his considerable musical skills, Sidey conducted his first evangelistic crusade for the Soul Winner's Association in June 1920 at Diamond Lake, Illinois. The publicity for the crusade (which he probably prepared) described Sidey as

> a man, who, while college trained, has evidently learned to think for himself. Although he has not yet acquired a reputation as a flowery orator, he has the faculty of forcefully presenting ideas that start and keep you thinking. His addresses are sure to be of uncommon interest to all those who enjoy the exercise of thought.[15]

The crusade was something of a disaster for Sidey who, because of his perceived inadequacies as an evangelist, felt a desperate need for "the baptism of power of the Holy Spirit."[16]

Disheartened and disillusioned by his first evangelistic crusade, Sidey decided to revitalize his faith and his ministry by attending a prophetic conference in Chicago. He and Edna were billeted at Moody Bible Institute, and while staying at Moody, Sidey discovered the influential premillennial tract, *The Second Coming of Christ*. Almost immediately Sidey and his wife saw their Christian faith in a radically new light. The imminent return of Christ, the rapture, the Moody-Scofield emphasis upon the dispensational view of the past, the present and future — all now made marvellous sense. Sidey discovered a new sense of purpose and direction in his life. It should not be surprising that Sidey's favorite verse from the Bible — and this tiny portion of the Scriptures would be eventually chiselled into his gravestone — came from 1 Thessalonians 4:16: "Waiting until the trumpet of the Lord shall sound."

Sidey, however, was not satisfied with merely waiting passively for the Lord to return. His premillennialism, in other words, did not immobilize him. He was determined to help prepare the way for Christ's return by preaching the gospel with zeal and conviction; moreover, he very much wanted to ensure that as many people as possible were, in fact, raptured before the terrible bloody battle of Armageddon.

In late 1920 and early 1921 a revitalized Sidey continued his work with the Soul Winner's Association of Illinois. His publicity brochure now had a somewhat different emphasis:

> Impressed by the vital need of spiritual life in the individuals who compose our civilization in this age, he with others, has decided to spend his life at the call of the Holy Spirit, in this tremendous field of evangelization. Mr. Sidey brings to the work a modern point of appeal of the Bible. The challenge "Back to the Bible" is the clarion call of his message. He believes in conversion, real regeneration, not handshaking or card-signing; but definite inquiry work followed by the witness of the Holy Spirit. On the other hand, the approach to all this is modern, not fanatical or highly emotional; simply an emphasis upon the Biblical spiritual realities as they have been shown to identify themselves with human nature.[17]

In a period of a few months, Sidey's essential gospel approach within the Soul Winner's Association had undergone a fundamental change.

There was now a concern about "conversion" and not about "ideas"; there was now an emphasis placed upon "back to the Bible" and the "witness of the Holy Spirit" and not, as had earlier been the case, with "the exercise of thought." Sidey had become a conservative evangelical; he was not yet, the evidence suggests, a fundamentalist. What seemed to separate these two positions was a certain degree of "violence in thought and language" which characterized the fundamentalist mind but not the conservative evangelical.[18] By late 1920, however, Sidey was certainly quickly moving in the fundamentalist direction — toward and beyond Moody Bible Institute and light years away from the University of Chicago Divinity School. The latter institution, for Sidey and his Chicago friends, had become the bastion of all the insidious and evil forces of modernism and liberalism then spreading across North America.

Despite the fact that she had two small children to be concerned about, Edna Sidey played a key role in her husband's two "Soul Winner's" evangelistic campaigns. She was a vigorous and dynamic woman, intelligent, shrewd and persuasive. She did not enjoy living in the United States and was therefore keen to return to her much-beloved Nova Scotia. When her husband's academic work had finally been completed at Union in 1921 and he had been ordained, she pressured him to return to her home in Burlington on the Avon River in Hants County. Soon after their return Sidey was baptized by immersion by the Reverend Neil Herman, minister of the Emmanuel Baptist Church, Truro. Sidey had met Herman, a leading Nova Scotia fundamentalist, in 1916, while spending a summer at Brunswick Street Methodist Church in Truro. (It is of some interest that one of the young boys taught by Sidey at the Brunswick Street Methodist Church was Robert Stanfield — a future premier of Nova Scotia and leader of the Progressive Conservative Party of Canada.)

II

For one reason or another Sidey showed little interest in finding a pastorate in a Methodist church in the province in 1921. Instead, he resolved to introduce into his adopted province an evangelistic approach he had learned with the Illinois "Soul Winners." His mission, as he saw it, was to bring the gospel of Christ to isolated backwaters of Nova Scotia. "The Soul Winner's Association of Nova Scotia" became an official branch of the Soul Winner's Association of Chicago.[19] At its first convention, held at Cambridge, Hants County, on July 1, 1922, a five-point program was agreed to concerning the work of the new association. First, it was stressed that the central thrust of the organization was "soul winning" in the rural, largely unchurched areas. Second, it was explicitly stated that the new group was interdenominational and a faith mission — that is, all financial support would come from concerned supporters. Third, "to encourage the study of the Bible, as it is written, without the aid of higher learning so-called," special "competitive examinations in Bible are held." Fourth, Sidey urged his followers to be completely dependent upon the "outpouring of the Holy Spirit," and fifth, not to forsake the "kindred fellowship with other Christians."[20]

Sidey organized a small team of dedicated workers, and by the spring and summer of 1922 he saw scores of people, especially in Hants County, converted to his brand of evangelical Christianity. In late 1922 and 1923 Sidey's "evangelistic band" travelled to Hammonds Plains, near Halifax, and then to the Eastern Shore and Guysborough County.[21] In the Jeddore area, Sidey's team worked very closely with local Baptists. One of the Eastern Shore residents wrote to Sidey on January 22, 1923:

> The work is still growing. Most every person you meet now has something to say about the goodness of God. The men who have gone away to the woods send us beautiful letters telling us how God stands by them in their temptations. There are temptations of all kinds. I am sure we can say God has blessed us in the work we have been doing. Every time we meet, we don't forget to pray for you people and hope to hear from you soon.[22]

On June 6, 1923, it was reported from Jeddore that the revival fires were still burning:

> I am so happy to know of such heavenly works being done. There has been a wonderful change in East Jeddore. I was down for a month [from Lunenburg] and it was to me the happiest month I have ever spent in my life. I really felt sorry when I had to leave them .... I said to Mother when I went home that it seemed everybody was better looking. Mother said, "That's happiness," and I thank God that through Mr. Sidey and his workers that this change has come.[23]

The 1922–23 Eastern Shore revival, which eventually spread into Guysborough County, was the means whereby hundreds of residents of a string of isolated settlements stretching from East Jeddore to Canso experienced the intensely satisfying and intensely pleasurable feeling of

Christian fellowship as the "ecstasy of spontaneous communitas" almost overwhelmed them. The "spontaneous communitas" produced by the Sidey team had something almost "magical about it." People, especially women who were attracted to the young, energetic, dynamic male preachers, almost despite their collective anxieties, shared a "feeling of endless power," and this all too rare feeling was both exhilarating and frightening. They were drawn by the "mystery of intimacy" towards one another, as Christian love challenged what appeared to be a selfish, limited and, indeed, almost worldly fidelity. They saw Christ in their friends and their neighbors, and they wanted desperately, even for a fleeting moment, to love their friends in the same way as they passionately loved their Christ. Some apparently did, for a brief moment, and their joy must have been remarkable. Then, as the flames of the revival died down, a number experienced what Victor Turner has called "the mystery of distancing and of tradition," and their intense feeling of Christian community — of oneness in the Lord — was shattered by sectarian strife and personality conflicts.[24]

In 1923 and 1924 in Guysborough County, Sidey received enthusiastic support from the Reverend E. W. Forbes, an influential Methodist minister located there. Forbes would remain close to Sidey throughout the campaign in which Sidey "preached 105 sermons (one every night) without a break and never preached the same sermon twice."[25] Yet despite the spiritual revivals he and his team had helped coax into existence, Sidey, by late 1924 and early 1925, was rather disillusioned with the work of the Nova Scotia Soul Winner's Association. Even the publishing of his own monthly newsletter *The Challenge*, which began in 1923, did not significantly affect Sidey's gnawing doubts about his evangelistic work. Sidey and his team realized that it was one thing to help people experience the "New Birth." Hundreds of Nova Scotians, and other Maritimers, they felt, had been converted in the 1922–24 period through the ministry of the Nova Scotia Soul Winner's Association. Yet once the team left the community, and once the revival ended, the new converts often found themselves without adequate spiritual nurturing, or else bitterly divided as to which church in the community was the true instrument of the Almighty. A disheartened and disillusioned Sidey observed that "my experience has taught me that, while God has given some pastors a greater gift as evangelists than others, yet, this office would be exercised as among brethren within the framework of the church or denomination to which such men adhere."[26]

After sacrificing four years of his life for his own creation, the Nova

Scotia Soul Winner's Association, Sidey had come to the conclusion in 1925 that he may have been wrong after all. His itinerating evangelistic work had apparently created more problems than it had resolved. He now understood why "Revival Meetings are often feared by many Christian pastors and leaders, who have to remain and face these things... wrangling when the evangelists have gone." For Sidey in 1925 it was far more important to "clearly define truth from error" than to organize evangelistic crusades which seemed to encourage the growth of "prejudice... jealousy and selfishness."[27]

It is not surprising therefore that in 1925 Sidey felt that the time was propitious for him to pastor a single church. He and his wife desired the stability, the regular income and the peace of mind that they hoped might come from a settled ministry. Moreover, he had lost faith in the efficacy of religious revivals — this point needs to be emphasized. Preaching 105 different sermons on 105 consecutive days was not something a normal father with a wife and two young children would want to do for the rest of his life. Nor was it something a *true* Christian pastor should do. As he entered his thirties, J. J. Sidey obviously needed a major change of pace; he, moreover, needed a church to pastor. But where might he find one? He could not return to the church of his father and the church in which he himself had been ordained, for Sidey was very much opposed to the creation of the United Church of Canada in 1925.

As he looked at his ministerial options in Nova Scotia, he saw few doors open to him. The United Church was out of the question. Its theology was too "modern" and its leadership too "liberal." Presbyterians opposed to Union had no desire to have him, nor did the Anglicans. What about the Baptists? Sidey had found that some of his most ardent supporters in the Soul Winner's Association were Maritime Baptists, but he also realized that the Convention leadership seemed to be controlled by the "Modernists." Nevertheless, the Reverend Neil Herman, a fundamentalist who had baptized him, urged him to join the Maritime Baptist Convention. The Reverend T. T. Shields, whom Sidey had first met in 1925, supported the pro-Baptist argument put forward by his friend Herman. Furthermore, it should not be forgotten that Sidey's wife was a Baptist, and she eagerly pushed her husband in the Baptist direction.

It should be kept in mind that Sidey had also conducted evangelistic campaigns in Prince Edward Island in 1923 and 1924 and had been particularly successful in the Bedeque area, so it should not be surprising that in 1925 the Central Bedeque United Baptist Church asked him to be their temporary supply minister. No other Baptist church in the Maritimes indicated any interest in "issuing a call" to Sidey, and for good reason. Sidey was an ordained Episcopal Methodist minister who had had no previous official contact with the Maritime Baptist Convention. He would therefore have to be satisfied with being a temporary supply minister in a tiny, peripheral, Convention church. He had to start somewhere. And Sidey and his wife were attracted by the bucolic charm of the "Garden of the Gulf." It would, among other things, be a good place to raise their children.

III

Sidey's less-than-five-year Bedeque sojourn, it may be argued, helped to transform him into an ardent fundamentalist. Fundamentalism's militant and extreme "opposition to modernism, both as a theology and a cultural secularity, distinguished it from earlier evangelical traditions,"[28] and as Ernest R. Sandeen[29] and George S. Marsden[30] have argued, fundamentalism in the early twentieth century in North America stressed the importance of certain distinctive beliefs — notably, premillennialism and the verbal inerrancy of the Bible as well as the revivalistic tradition of D. L. Moody and Common Sense philosophy as it applied to theological and scientific truth. In addition, its belief core included a largely traditional Calvinist theology and an emphasis on the substitutionary atonement theory and the pure church ideal. For Sidey, the inerrancy of the Scriptures, substitutionary atonement and premillennialism would be the most important fundamentalist tenets.

While at Bedeque, Sidey became very closely associated with the controversial Reverend J. J. Daggett, minister at the nearby Tryon United Baptist Church. Until Daggett's death in 1939, he would be Sidey's confidant, aide and intimate friend. A native of Grand Manan Island, Daggett, who was educated briefly at Colby College, Maine, and the University of New Brunswick, was ordained in 1894 as a Free Christian Baptist minister. He played a key role in pushing the somewhat reluctant New Brunswick Free Christian Baptists into union in 1905 with the much larger Regular or Calvinist Maritime Baptist Church. Daggett left the United Baptist ministry in 1911 to become a deputy minister in the New Brunswick Department of Agriculture. He served in this capacity until 1917, when he was implicated in the notorious Valley Railroad and Potato Scandal. It was charged, among other things, that Daggett had not only been the conduit for transferring large sums of money into and out of the hands of Conservative Party supporters, but also had lied during the McQueen Commission hearings held in 1918.[31] Driven from the Department of Agriculture, Daggett served as pastor of the Marysville, New Brunswick, United Baptist Church, until being called to the Tryon, P.E.I., United Baptist Church. Here he ministered until 1926, when he moved to the Kingston, Nova Scotia, United Baptist pastorate.

Sidey and Daggett were a remarkable team. In many respects very different, their respective strengths complemented one another and made each of them — when in tandem — more powerful and influential individuals. Certainly, when Daggett was living near him, Sidey was a far more aggressive and closed-minded individual. Daggett helped greatly in making Sidey "the Combatant."

Sidey was a tall and robust man, full of vigor and seldom sick. His "penetrating grey-blue eyes"[32] were often full of fun, and he loved to laugh. Daggett, on the other hand, was sickly, small in stature and very serious. Unlike Sidey, who carefully hid his emotions from public view, Daggett was a feisty, peppery individual, whose quick temper often manifested itself in cutting remarks. He was, it has been accurately observed, "a fighter by nature"[33] and like many others who have also suffered from tuberculosis, he was very mercurial and, some would say, a kind of manic-depressive.

Even before Sidey had had time to settle into his new Bedeque charge, he found himself a principal actor in the creation of the Maritime Christian Fundamentalist Association. All Maritimers interested in battling against modernism were invited to a special conference held in Truro in August 1925. The Truro Fundamentalist Conference was hosted by the Immanuel United Baptist Church, and the guest speaker was T. T. Shields, the so-called "Spurgeon of Canada" and in the 1920s Canada's leading fundamentalist. He had already helped to split the Ontario and Quebec Baptist Convention into two warring factions — a split that would be formalized a few years later.

At the conference, it has been suggested, Shield's was certain that he had been inspired — in singling out Sidey — "to groom God's man for His job in the Maritimes."[34] Moreover, much to the satisfaction of Shields, a key resolution was adopted that

> this meeting having a clear understanding of the issues involved, and realizing that the fundamentals of the gospel are in danger of being obscured in these days, through the widespread acceptance of modern ideas of the Bible, does hereby register its protest, and propose that an organization for the purpose of spreading information as to the real issues involved be formed and shall be known as *The*

Maritime Christian Fundamentalist Association.[35]

Daggett was elected the interim president of the new association and Sidey, the interim secretary.

The two Island ministers, spurred on by Shields, planned a special Conference on Christian Fundamentals to be held at Tryon United Baptist Church, Prince Edward Island, on November 3–5, 1925. It was hoped that this conference would attract all interested fundamentalists from a wide spectrum of Maritime churches. The main speaker for the conference was the Reverend Edward Morris, Rector of St. Matthias Anglican Church, Halifax, and a committed premillennialist. A graduate of Wycliffe College, the University of Toronto, Morris had become the Maritime spokesman of the Scofield dispensational point of view.

Morris did not breathe much life in the Maritime Christian Fundamentalist Association, however. In fact, by January 1926 the organization was dead. Why? Why had it died after a life of only a few months of existence? Was it because of ineffective leadership? Or was it because there was very little ministerial interest in the organization? Obviously there was little apparent interest! Was it because the administrative elite of the leading Protestant denominations conspired to destroy the organization before it threatened the spiritual hegemony of what has been called by one of Sidey's supporters "the echelon of the denominational circles"?[36] Probably not. It is hard to see how the fundamentalist association hoped to expand from their tiny Baptist base in Prince Edward Island. They needed leadership and support from the New Brunswick and Nova Scotia Baptist mainstream as well as from key sectors of the United Church, the Presbyterian Church and the Anglicans. In 1925 the United and Presbyterian churches had other more important things to worry about, and the few evangelical Anglicans were not eager to join an organization dominated by premillennialists and what they must have regarded as bush-league Baptists. Most Maritime United Baptist Convention clergy saw no need for such an organization. Their denomination was considered to be more than sympathetic to the fundamentalist cause any way. Some of them, moreover, must have had some serious reservations about the leadership of Sidey and Daggett — two outsiders, and one with an unsavory reputation indeed.

The sudden collapse of the Maritime Christian Fundamentalist Association meant that Sidey had much more time and energy to devote to his Bedeque church and to the Maritime United Baptist Convention. Perhaps the Convention and not an interdenominational fundamentalist association would be the God-given means to protect the Christian church from the growing modernist bombardment. In 1926 Sidey officially became a Baptist — becoming a member of the Central Bedeque United Baptist Church. The following year his church asked the Convention Examining Council for Ordination that "their Pastor Rev. J. J. Sidey, formerly a regularly ordained minister of the Methodist Episcopal body, but now a member of the Bedeque Church, be registered as a regularly ordained Baptist Minister." Sidey, together with a former Seventh-Day Adventist minister, was examined by the Council for Ordination. After hearing "a frank statement" of his "doctrinal views," and after "careful consideration," the Council resolved that Sidey's name "be added to our official list."[37] He was listed as "Sidey, J. J., M.A. D.D. Central Bedeque, 1927."[38]

Within six years, however, Sidey had left the Maritime United Baptist Convention. From his fundamentalist stronghold at Kingston, Nova Scotia, where he had moved in 1929, he had attempted to split the Convention into warring fundamentalist and liberal factions. In this attempt he had largely failed. He was only successful in persuading a handful of Baptist churches to follow him out of the Convention. Yet despite his disappointment at not becoming the "T. T. Shields of the Maritimes," Sidey nevertheless was responsible for establishing the Kingston Bible College in 1934 as well as his own publication, *The Gospel Light*, in 1931. In addition, in 1935 the interdenominational International Christian Mission was created by Sidey with its own monthly, *The Question*.

IV

By late 1935, Sidey had come to realize that his attempt to split the Maritime Baptist Convention had failed, yet he refused to be immobilized and disoriented by the events of 1934 and 1935. He seemed even more enthusiastic about his Kingston area churches, more committed to his Bible college and the International Christian Mission. Sidey, moreover, became increasingly active in the Nova Scotia Sons of Temperance as well as the Canadian Protestant League.

Despite his energy and sense of commitment, Sidey was not able to deal successfully with the forces of sectarianism he had helped to unleash in the Kingston area. His college, for example, experienced a number of painful schisms as faculty members left, outraged at Sidey's enthusiasm for pentecostalism, one year, or his obsession with British Israelitism during another. Some of his Independent Baptist followers stubbornly refused to toe his line and attacked his college and the I.C.M. because they were not

Baptist organizations. By 1939 most of the Nova Scotia Independent Baptist churches had split away from Sidey. It was ironic that Sidey should experience a far worse split in the 1930s than did the Convention, yet he had played a key role in organizing the Independent Baptist churches in the Cape Sable area of Shelburne County, in Guysborough County and in Westchester, Cumberland County, as well as in the Bedeque area of Prince Edward Island.

When Sidey formed the Maritime Fellowship of Independent Baptists in 1940, he could only attract to the organization his Kingston-area Independent Baptist and the tiny Coddle Harbour Baptist churches from Guysborough County. The purpose of the new organization was:

1. To provide a way whereby the Baptists (Ind.) of the Maritime Provinces may find fellowship together.
2. To promote Baptist (Ind.) work in the Maritime Provinces.
3. To provide a way whereby Baptist (Ind.) may form a united stand upon any issue that may affect them, either as Christians or as Baptists (Ind.).[39]

In September 1968 the Fellowship was formally disbanded; Sidey had been in no position to keep a fragile Fellowship together. In 1962 his own Melvern Square Independent Church had split, with the secessionist group associating itself with the Fellowship of Evangelical Baptist Churches. Four years later, Sidey, a spent force, died. He had seen his Independent Baptist world collapse around him; his college was still in reasonable shape despite a tragic fire in 1962, but his I.C.M. was little more than a postal address — a paper missionary society.

Soon after Sidey's death on May 23, 1966, he was described by one of his faithful deacons and dear friend, E. E. Skaling from Greenwood, in the following manner: "Dr. Sidey was not perfect. He has weaknesses, the chief of which may have been his lack of understanding of the financial world; but he was a man of faith, a man who knew how to get answers to prayer, a good friend and a Christian gentleman."[40]

J. J. Sidey in the 1930s, it may be argued, represented the way the mainstream of the Maritime Baptists could have, but did not, follow. His career tells us a great deal about the fundamentalist-modernist struggle in the three Maritime provinces — perhaps providing the best available lens through which to view the ongoing struggle between the two ideologies. Sidey's career, however, tells us more than this. It also appears to provide some proof, especially for the early 1920s, that the revivalist tradition in the region was not yet completely dead. Sidey was obviously no Henry Alline; yet in the early 1920s, without question, he was very much an integral part of the Allinite–New Light tradition. His bitter abandonment of "revivalism" after 1925, however, suggests that the Allinite tradition was indeed dying, if not dead, at least in Nova Scotia. And Sidey's enthusiastic espousal of fundamentalism and his sustained offensive against experiential religion in the 1925–1966 period only confirmed the death of the New Light tradition. Obsessed with defending themselves from the strident fundamentalist attacks of Sidey and his disciples, Maritime Baptists found little time or energy to evangelize — as Harris Harding once expressed it in 1792 — "with one foot on Ebal and the other on Gerazim in the name of the Lord, and deliver Eternal decrees and Messages to Saints and Sinners."[41]

Epilogue

Since the latter part of the nineteenth century, revivalism has not been a crucially important formative force in Canadian religious life. When sustained religious revivals have occurred in the twentieth century, for example, they have usually taken place in peripheral regions — like the isolated Eastern Shore of Nova Scotia in the early 1920s or northern Saskatchewan in the 1970s. In a sense, these twentieth-century revivals were nineteenth-century social movements affecting local communities and often the result of a powerful symbiotic relationship linking preachers and an "agitated" community "swelling and raging like a sea in a storm."[1]

Why was the cutting edge of Canadian revivalism significantly dulled by so-called modernity? The distinguished Princeton theologian J. Gresham Machen said in September 1912: "We may preach with all the fervour of a reformer and yet succeed only in winning a straggler here and there, if we permit the whole collective thought of a nation or of the world to be controlled by ideas which, by the relentless force of logic, prevent Christianity from being regarded as anything more than a harmless delusion."[2] As far as Machen was concerned, these pernicious "ideas" were Christian modernism, and he was convinced that modernism was destroying the essential fundamentals of the true Christian faith. Most Canadian fundamentalists in the twentieth century and most Canadian liberals would have endorsed Machen's contention. In fact, this Whig interpretation of the decline of evangelical Christianity in Canada in "Late Victorian Canada" and beyond has now become the standard version of Canadian historiography. In Ramsay Cook's prize-winning volume, *The Regenerators: Social Criticism in Late Victorian English Canada* (Toronto, 1985), it is implicitly and explicitly argued that profound doubt triggered by Darwinism and biblical higher criticism led to the secularization of Canadian evangelicalism and the transformation of pietism into an essentially social religion.

Census data appears to support this contention. During the last fifty years, for example, the fastest-growing religious group in Canada has been that which defines itself as having "No religion." In 1981, 7.2 percent of the Canadian population located themselves in this category — 1,752,380

Canadians out of a total population of 24,083,495. (See Chart A at end of chapter.) The number of Canadians with "No religion" was, it should be noted, larger than the combined number of *all* Canadian Baptists and Presbyterians. And in British Columbia in 1981, the largest religious group in the province, making up 20.5 percent of the population, was the "No Religion" one. (See Chart B at end of chapter.) If there is a religious revival occurring in contemporary Canada, it may be argued, it is a revival which is transforming thousands of nominal Canadian Christians into non-believers.

There is yet another way to look at the apparent decline of Canadian revivalism and of Canadian evangelicalism during the past century. It may be argued that the evangelical consensus and revivalistic religion were not necessarily battered into supine nothingness from outside by Darwinism and higher criticism. Rather, the evangelical consensus disintegrated from within as evangelical Christianity lost its collective soul to North American consumerism — the insidious antithesis to essential Christianity. The simple Christian message based upon self-abnegation and sacrifice was replaced by the narcissistic gospel of intense "therapeutic self-realization."[3] By the last two decades of the nineteenth century, it has been recently observed, "the leaders of the W.A.S.P. bourgeoisie felt cramped . . . over-civilized . . . cut off from real life — threatened from without by an ungrateful working-class, and from within by their own sense of physical atrophy and spiritual decay."[4] Moreover,

> the old religious sanctions for the moral life, a life of sacrifice and toil, had begun to disintegrate . . . A crisis of purpose, a yearning for a solid, transcendent framework of meaning, was not just Henry Adams' worry, but that of a much wider group. In this time of cultural consternation, the new professional-managerial corps appeared with a timely dual message. On the one hand, they preached a new morality that substantiated the old goal of transcendence to new ideals of self-fulfillment and immediate gratification. The late nineteenth-century link between individual hedonism and bureaucratic organization — a link that has been strengthened in the twentieth century — marks the point of departure of a modern American consumer culture. The consumer culture is not only the value-system that underlies a society saturated by mass-produced and mass-marketed goods, but also a new set of sanctions for the elite control of that society.[5]

This inner transformation of both North American society and Protestantism is of crucial importance to any sophisticated understanding of late nineteenth century and twentieth-century Canadian revivalism. Consumerism, in a profound sense, cut the essential heart out of the evangelical consensus and out of revivalism. The marriage between "individual hedonism" and "bureaucratic organization" was especially noticeable in the so-called modern revivalistic tradition. Here, the linking of the two produced not only a largely superficial narcissistic therapeutic gospel but also one profoundly affected by misogyny and male clerical control. No longer would revivals be community outpourings of guilt and the resolution of guilt, of broken relationships being rebuilt and renewed, of shared intense "communitas" shaped by women, children and men. With the professionalization of the evangelical male clergy came control from the top down and a deep suspicion of popular religious movements which they could not manipulate — especially movements involving women. It should never be forgotten that, as Tom Harpur has recently pointed out, "from one very important point of view, the whole of organized religion is a not-too-subtle form of power-seeking and control."[6] Thus the symbiotic link between community and preacher was snapped, and in the process the revival became a largely empty shell, devoid of intense, transforming Christian ecstasy.

It must be re-emphasized that in the long and in the short run, North American consumerism had a far greater negative impact on the late nineteenth century evangelical consensus than did the various manifestations of so-called modern scholarship. At the centre of this inner decay, as D. W. Frank has recently contended, was the cancer of consumerism — "based on self-indulgence."[7] The testimony of an American woman visiting some eighty years ago a department store, the key economic institution of the consumer society, cuts to the heart of the issue:

I felt myself overcome little by little by a disorder that can only be compared to that of drunkenness, with the dizziness and excitation that are peculiar to it. I saw things as if through a cloud, everything stimulated my desire and assumed, for me, an extraordinary attraction. I felt myself swept along toward them and I grabbed hold of things without any outside and superior consideration intervening to hold me back. Moreover I took things at random, useless and worthless articles as well as useful and expensive articles. It was like a monomania of possession.[8]

Other women made similar comments — "My head was spinning," "I felt completely dizzy," "I am just as if I were drunk." These comments were made by middle-class women who had been arrested for shoplifting. They were, it has been observed, "an odd foreshadowing of Billy Sunday's contention that alcohol was the cause of virtually all crime." The women's addiction, however, was "to consumer gratification." "The pathological frenzy to which some women were driven," it is clear, "had become simply the seamier side of the new consumer society, where the old virtues of thrift and self-control were giving way to a culture of gratification."[9] These women, drunk on goods, were striking symbols of the new consumer society.

It was virtually impossible for evangelical leaders in the post-1880 period to attack frontally the insidious anti-Christian bias of consumerism. Instead, they became its ardent disciples and enthusiastic advocates of the fundamental goodness of economic growth and technological development. They were certainly unwilling to see what Karl Marx saw in "modern bourgeois society" in the 1880s and beyond. For Marx, such a society "has conjured up such gigantic means of production and of exchange" that it has in the process become "like the sorcerer who is no longer able to control the powers of the subterranean which he has called up by his spells." Marx then went on:

> Constant revolutionizing of production, uninterrupted disturbance of all social relations, everlasting uncertainty and agitation, distinguish the bourgeois epoch from all earlier ones. All fixed, fast-frozen relations, with their train of ancient and venerable prejudices and opinions, are swept away, all new-formed ones become antiquated before they can ossify. All that is solid melts into air, all that is holy is profane.[10]

Marx had lain bare the essential nature of life in modernizing society, and he had intuitively realized what had happened to North American evangelicalism. The "holy" had in a profound sense become "profane," and all that was "solid" had melted into nothingness.

Few, if any, Canadian evangelicals in the late nineteenth century and early twentieth century would have or, more accurately, could have accepted the validity of Marx's penetrating prophetic insight into the essential nature of bourgeois-industrial society. Yet, as the nineteenth century blurred into the twentieth, a number of evangelicals came to realize that something fundamentally destructive was beginning to undermine the theological and ideological underpinnings of their church and their society. But instead of focusing, as Marx had done, on the distinguishing features of the "bourgeois society" or as others had done on the evils of "consumerism," these disconcerted evangelicals concentrated their concern on what to them was theological modernism — the way in which Darwinian scientific progress and biblical scholarship was significantly altering the older evangelical consensus. Many of these evangelicals would become known as fundamentalists, and their growing obsession with preserving theological purity would be matched by a remarkable degree of "violence in thought and language."[11] These people would find it far easier to be judgmental than forgiving, destructive rather than constructive and confrontational rather than accommodative. They were so concerned with defending what they felt was the pristine purity of Christianity that some had little time and energy to reach out and to evangelize the unchurched. The fundamentalists were apparently content to encourage what has been aptly called the "Circulation of the Saints"[12] rather than unstructured revivalistic outreach. They needed to control everything — the past, the present and the future, and their growing preoccupation with premillennial dispensationalism only underscored the fact that having lost control of contemporary North American society, they were even more determined to control the future.

Those North American revivalists who reached out in the twentieth century to the unconverted did so largely as prophets of religious consumerism. Salvation, for a Billy Sunday, the great early twentieth century American evangelist, who often visited Canada, was a very, very simple matter, and a person "can be converted without any fuss."[13] For Sunday, moreover, as one of his disciples expressed it, "religion loses whatever traits of feminity it may have possessed, before the Sunday campaign is over."[14] The revival had become a simple, male-dominated consumer response, "without any fuss," to be used by the best religious salesman in the community. Cheap grace, emptied of sacrifice, commitment and a deep suspicion of contemporary values, had become the "thin veneer over an increasingly secularized and consumer-oriented product."[15] Television evangelism, in the post–World War II period, became the most sophisticated purveyor of this "product." Is it surprising that as the twentieth century unfolded, Canadian life at every level of experience was increasingly Americanized, and Canadian religious values began to reflect so slavishly those being created at the centre of the consumerism's empire?

At one time Canadian revivalists and revivals openly challenged the status quo; they frontally attacked the values of contemporary society, and they encouraged and facilitated the growth of a sense of community. During the revivals, women, men and children were all one in Christ and were seen as spiritual equals. Of course, revivals were followed by declension, and many who had had mountain-peak experiences found themselves soon after the embers had cooled in the depths of spiritual despair. Yet for a moment — and for some an eternity — they had been almost magically drawn together as a people of God. Then, perhaps because they were so human, they could not endure in a "spirit of brokenness, confession and repentance."[16] It was so difficult for them to be satisfied with Christ and to resonate with Jacques Ellul that "beyond Jesus, beyond him there is nothing — nothing but lies."[17]

In the twentieth century, however, much of what would be preached by the new prophets of evangelical consumerism would in fact be "nothing but lies," and the decline in importance of Canadian revivalism in the late nineteenth century and the twentieth century, may, in fact, be a significant religious statement. Instead of being attracted to what is seen as the hypocrisy of the Christian gospel, and revolted by the spiritual hubris of fundamentalism, tens of thousands of Canadians are satisfied with abandoning Christianity completely. This may be the most important religious movement in Canada in the 1980s and the 1990s. And rather than weakening the true evangelical impulse in Canada, this movement may, in an ironic manner, be responsible for revitalizing a tradition — an evangelical tradition which in the twentieth century has been largely denuded of Christlike love by a myriad of confused prophets.

Afterword

Even a superficial reading of this book will discern the influence of Anthony Wallace, Victor Turner and George Marsden. Sometimes Wallace's influence seems to be of primary and explicit importance, and sometimes Turner's. And then there is George Marsden's implicit influence — almost everywhere — and nowhere is it recognized explicitly. But despite what to some might be my growing dependence on Wallace and Turner, I hope that I have not been shackled by their work or in any way intellectually stultified. I have attempted to use their insights with care, and usually for descriptive rather than analytical purposes. I have mixed their often brilliant themes of religious change together and added some of my own interpretations to produce, I hope, a novel way of looking at revivals and revivalists.

. According to Wallace, a religious revitalization movement — or, in other words, a revival — occurs "when a society finds its day-to-day behavior has deviated so far from the accepted (traditional) norms that neither individuals nor large groups can honestly (consistently) sustain the common set of religious understandings by which they believe (have been taught) they should act." A period of "individual stress" — or loss of identity — is followed by one of "cultural distortion" during which the "ordinary stress reduction techniques fail to help those who react to them." Then there arises a charismatic leader or leaders, people who have undergone the traumatic religious experience "that epitomizes the crisis of the culture." Such leaders, in the fourth stage of the revitalization movement, "begin to attract the more flexible (usually the younger) members of the society, who are willing to experiment with new mazeways or lifestyles." There is often a collective pulling back or retreat to an explicit conservative-negative position and then a sudden leap forward to a new and seemingly radically different "world view." Finally, the revivalists succeed in influencing the more passive individuals — and as the collective "mazeways are cleared ... familiar patterns change, sex roles alter," and a new and revitalized culture clicks into fragile place. It is a religious culture shaped both by the past and the present, and the process repeats itself, in somewhat different form, as groups in each generation attempt to revitalize their way of life.[1]

At the core of the Wallace thesis is to be found an emphasis on what the sociologist Seymour M. Lipset has referred to as the need for people under stress to find "a dynamic equilibrium" between what has been referred to as "autonomous action and changing experiences."[2] And consequently, for Wallace and his disciples,

> a religious revival or a great awakening begins when accumulated pressures for change produce such acute personal and social stress that the whole culture must break the crust of custom, crash through the blocks in the mazeways, and find new socially structured avenues along which the members of the society may pursue their course in mutual harmony with one another.[3]

And for Wallace, the charismatic "prophet" leads the way towards the "dynamic equilibrium." That individual

> reveals (as God's chosen messenger) this new way to his fellow men. Gradually he develops a band of disciples or followers, whom he appoints (or anoints) and they fan out through the social system to proselytize for the new religious order. Among the precepts they inculcate are not only theological statements regarding the nature and will of God and how he is to be worshipped but also (more or less explicitly) a new set of social norms for individual and group behaviour. Those who come in contact with the prophet or his charismatic disciples are "touched" by the same divine experience, and this validates both the prophet's vision and the new mazeways he inculcates as God's will for his people.[4]

The "charisma" of the prophet or prophetess and his or her disciples is not necessarily only an extraordinarily powerful "attribute of individual personality or a mystical quality." There is an important "social relationship" involved in "charisma" as well.[5] As far as the influential sociologist Peter Worsley is concerned, charisma, in fact, provides much "more than an abstract ideological rationale." It is, he argues, stretching Wallace yet a little further,

> a legitimization grounded in a relationship of loyalty and identification in which the leader is followed simply because he embodies values in which the followers have an "interest" ... The follow-

ers ... in a dialectical way, create, by selecting them out, the leaders who in turn *command* on the basis of this newly-accorded legitimacy ... He articulates and consolidates their aspirations.[6]

The Wallace paradigm, as far as I was concerned, seemed especially valuable when applied to Henry Alline and Nova Scotia's First Great Awakening. The Wallace revitalization thesis, it should be stressed, was not used simplistically to explain all aspects of the widespread social movement which engulfed what is now Nova Scotia and New Brunswick during the American Revolution. Rather, I found that the insights which Wallace provided, largely from his study *The Death and Rebirth of the Seneca* (N.Y. 1970), but also in his seminal article "Revitalization Movements" (*American Anthropology* 58 [1956], pp. 264–281), could be carefully used to throw light on Henry Alline, his message and the remarkable impact he had on Nova Scotia and northern New England. Thus, for me, Wallace's revitalization thesis was more or less a descriptive device rather than an explanatory one, and, moreover, it provided me with the opportunity to locate my reassessment of Alline within the context of Wallace's influential thesis. In other words, and to be disconcertingly blunt, my *Ravished by the Spirit: Religious Revivals, Baptists and Henry Alline* (Montreal, 1984) was an attempt to associate my work closely with that of Wallace and W. G. McLoughlin, the author of *Revivals, Awakenings and Reform* (Chicago, 1978), a historian very much influenced by Wallace. This was not — I hoped — an example of guilt by association, but rather possible relevance and importance by association. I was eager to locate my work on what I considered to be the leading edge of American religious scholarship. Since most Canadian scholars remained uninterested in what I was doing, I looked longingly southward, both for inspiration and recognition. Perhaps this was a mistake, perhaps it was not.

I further strengthened my growing dependence on American ideological constructs by using the work of Victor Turner in much the same way I was using Anthony Wallace's revitalization thesis. Wallace, for me, threw considerable light on Alline and his disciples and the role they played in triggering scores of revivals in the Maritimes during and after the American Revolution. But as I moved into the post-Alline period, Wallace seemed to become increasingly irrelevant as I was confronted more and more by the question: Why were so many ordinary Nova Scotians and New Brunswickers in the first three or four decades of the nineteenth century — the time of the so-called Second Awakening — so greatly affected by evangelical religion as it was manifested in a series of intense religious revivals which swept the region? I was tempted to appropriate the "social control" model which Paul Johnson appeared to use so effectively in *A Shopkeeper's Millennium: Society and Revivals in Rochester, New York, 1815-1837* (N.Y., 1978).

Yet, when I tried to apply the "social control" model to Yarmouth, Nova Scotia, in the first decade of the nineteenth century or to Liverpool, Nova Scotia, at the same time, or to other Maritime communities in the 1820s and 1830s as they were convulsed by religious revivals, I saw that "social control" made no sense whatsoever. There was no evidence that members of a middle or an upper class in these communities were using religious revivals to protect their increasingly threatened interests. In fact, the evidence suggested quite the opposite — that the revivals were viewed by the Maritime elite as being almost revolutionary threats to the status quo. They tended to equate revivalism with American and later French republicanism, and they did everything in their power to eradicate what they disparagingly referred to as "New Light Fanaticism."[7] Bishop Charles Inglis of Nova Scotia cogently expressed what he knew to be the Maritime elite establishment view in April 1799. Inglis wrote:

> Fanatics are impatient under civil restraint & run into the demo-
> cratic system. They are for leveling everything both sacred and civil;
> & this is peculiarly the case of our New Lights [the disciples of Henry
> Alline] who are, as far as I can learn, Democrats to a man.[8]

The Inglis view, it is clear, would prevail for much of the pre-Confederation period.

If the Johnston "social control" model was, as it has been recently argued and as I had found, totally "obsolete,"[9] then it seemed reasonable for me to accept passively, as a given, the biting anticipated critique of my neo-Marxist scholar friends and disregard it and to look seriously at Victor Turner instead. This I did during my 1982/3 sabbatical at Harvard University. I tried to read all that I could find written by Turner, and I religiously attended one of his public lectures at Harvard.

I began to realize that Turner, especially in *The Ritual Process: Structure and Anti-Structure* (Ithaca, 1979), had provided me with a possible explanatory and descriptive framework in which I could locate the popular evangelical response to revivals and revivalists in the Maritimes in the early nineteenth century. What I had found lacking in Wallace and McLoughlin I discovered often in literary form in Turner.

Through the lens provided by *The Ritual Process*, I began to see late eighteenth and early nineteenth century revivals in particular as special "rituals" whereby, as Turner had brilliantly suggested, "well-bonded" human beings had created "by structural means — spaces and times in the calendar or, in the cultural cycles of their most cherished groups which cannot be captured" in what he has called the "classificatory nets of their routinized spheres of action." By "verbal and non-verbal means," religious revivals became the means whereby huge numbers of Maritimers and Canadians were able to break away from their "innumerable constraints and boundaries" and capture what Turner has called the "floating world" of self-discovery and inner freedom and actualization. Everyone, according to Turner, alternates between so-called "fixed" and "floating" worlds. They oscillate, in other words, between, on the one hand, preoccupation with order and constraint and, on the other hand, a search for novelty and freedom.

Thus, for thousands of Canadians, revivals were the occasion to experience first-hand and with intensity what has been termed an "antistructural liminality." The religious revival thus became the actual social means whereby all sorts of complex and hitherto internalized and sublimated desires, dreams, hopes and aspirations became legitimized. Often, traditional behavior and values were openly challenged; and the "antistructural liminality" of the revival ritual helped to give shape and form, however transitory, to a profoundly satisfying "tender, silent, cognizant mutuality." Often, seemingly aberrant behavior, such as women and children exhorting publicly that their husbands and fathers needed to be converted, became "rituals of status reversal." "Cognitively," as Turner points out, "nothing underlines regularity as well as absurdity or paradox," and emotionally nothing satisfies as much as extravagant or temporarily permitted illicit behaviour." Grown men could openly weep during a revival; this was widely perceived as a sign of grace and not a sign of weakness. Married women could in public chastise their husbands during the revival — this abandoning of deference was simply seen as the acceptable work of the Holy Spirit as was the often intense criticism by children of their unchristian and worldly parents.

According to Turner, there is in the ritual process an intensely satisfying and intensely pleasurable feeling of fellowship — as the "ecstasy of spontaneous communitas" virtually overwhelms everyone involved directly and indirectly in the ritual process in general and the revival in particular. What Turner calls the "spontaneous communitas" produced by rituals like revivals had something almost "magical" about it. People, almost despite themselves, shared, for what seemed eternity but was really a fragile moment, a "feeling of endless power." And this feeling was both exhilarating and frightening. When applied specifically to revivals, this bonding — this so-called "mystery of intimacy" — drew people, men and women and children, toward one another as Christian love triggered by the revival challenged what seemed to be a selfish, circumscribed, almost worldly, fidelity. They saw Christ in their friends and their neighbors and they wanted ever so desperately to love their friends as they loved their Christ. Some apparently did — or so they wrote — and their joy must have been intense as they looked at the world from the mountain-peak of religious ecstasy. Then they realized, often to their bitter sorrow, that "spontaneous communitas" was only a "phase, a moment, not a permanent condition" as the reality of "distancing and of tradition" regained firm control in the community. But it was always a return to the status quo with a difference; for people had behaved differently during the revival, and some people had been permanently changed. Some would never replicate their mountain-peak religious experience. Others would, as religious revivals became the means whereby their Christian faith was often both renewed, and revitalized.[10]

The "ecstasy of spontaneous communitas" and the "mystery of intimacy" were two crucially important and common themes I had perceived in a series of late eighteenth and early nineteenth century revivals I had examined in some detail in the early 1980s. Turner's *Ritual Process* gave me the academic courage to pursue my work on Maritime revivals from the bottom up rather than from the top down and from inside rather than from outside, or at least I wished to move in this direction despite the fact that often I lacked what one reviewer of *Ravished by the Spirit* referred to as the necessary demographic and statistical data to support my generalizations. Unfortunately, the data for so-called "thick history"[11] was not readily available, particularly for the late eighteenth and early nineteenth centuries. As one moved into the nineteenth century, however, one found more and more material which one could use to reconstruct revivals from the bottom up and from inside out.

It is noteworthy that this has been attempted for the Great Yarmouth Revival of 1827–28 by D. C. Goodwin. Goodwin, in his M.A. thesis, "Advancing Light: Evangelicalism in Yarmouth Township 1761-1830," written at Acadia University in 1986, is critical of *Ravished by the Spirit*, arguing that its author "failed to produce detailed studies of the religious development in specific churches to support his arguments."[12] Of course Goodwin is quite right, but it is noteworthy that his anatomy of the Yarmouth Revival of 1827–28 is largely one-dimensional and rather limited. He does make some use of the Yarmouth census data, and he does show that 51 percent of the 326 Baptist converts were men and 49 percent women. Of the men, some 16 percent were farmers, 19.8 percent seamen and 18.6 percent artisans; 87.5 percent were married and 12.5 percent unmarried. Of the women converts, 40.7 percent were unmarried and 59.3 percent married. But what do these figures really tell us about why people were converted? They may tell us a great deal, but how does one squeeze them to obtain this kind of information? Goodwin, at least, is pointing in the right direction, and his specific community revival study should encourage further work not only in the area of Nova Scotia revivalism but also that of Canadian revivalism. There have been too many generalizations about Canadian revivals — many of them made in my work — and too little careful historical analysis of those specific communities affected by the revivals during the past two centuries.

Certainly, some of the Goodwin critique of my *Ravished by the Spirit* is valid, and this point needs to be underscored, yet even Goodwin has to admit that the "four chapters were originally given as lectures at the 1983 Hayward Lectures at Acadia University where time would not have permitted the inclusion of more extensive evidence."[13] Goodwin could also have mentioned that the essential thrust of my Hayward Lectures was to try to explain why revivalism had become less and less important for Maritime Baptists in the latter half of the nineteenth century and the early part of the twentieth century. In addition, he could have pointed out that my lectures were, in a sense, jeremiads in which I attempted to address the remarkable declension of the Maritime Baptists in the twentieth century. Furthermore, the point could also have been made that in *Ravished by the Spirit* I was preoccupied with trying to find out why revivals actually occurred. What were the situational pressures which apparently triggered these "spiritual earthquakes" — as Richard Bushman has called them?[14] Had I been accurate in my earlier work in placing heavy emphasis on socio-psychological factors? For example, as late as 1976 I wrote the following about Henry Alline and Nova Scotia's First Great Awakening:

> Henry Alline was one Nova Scotian who was able to perceive a special purpose for his fellow colonists in the midst of the confused Revolutionary situation. He was the charismatic leader of the intense religious revival which swept the colony during the war period. The revival was not merely a "retreat from the grim realities of the world to the safety and pleasantly exciting warmth of the revival meeting," and "to profits and rewards of another character." Nor was it

basically 'a revolt of the outsettlements against Halifax or an irrational outburst against all forms of traditionalism and authority.
The Great Awakening of Nova Scotia may be viewed as an attempt
by many Yankee inhabitants to appropriate a new sense of identity
and a renewed sense of purpose. Religious enthusiasm in this context, a social movement of profound consequence in the Nova
Scotian situation, was symptomatic of a kind of collective identity
crisis as well as a searching for an acceptable and meaningful ideol-
ogy. Resolution of the crisis came not only when the individuals
were absorbed into what they felt was a dynamic fellowship of true
believers but also when they accepted Alline's analysis of contemporary events and his conviction that their colony was the centre of a
crucial cosmic struggle . . .

The implication of the conjunction of events of civil war in
New England and an outpouring of the Holy Spirit in Nova Scotia
was obvious to Alline and the thousands who flocked to hear him.
God was passing New England's historical mantle of Christian
leadership to Nova Scotia . . . In the world view of those New Englanders fighting for the Revolutionary cause, Old England was
corrupt and the Americans were engaged in a righteous and noble
cause. There was therefore some meaning for hostilities. But to
Alline the totally "inhuman War" had no such meaning. Rather,
along with all the other signs of the times, it could only indicate one
thing, that the entire Christian world, apart from Nova Scotia, was
abandoning the way of God.[15]

By the early 1980s, however, I had come increasingly to realize that
there probably was something more in the First Great Awakening than the
mere resolving of the collective identity crisis of Nova Scotians. This did
not of course mean that I enthusiastically abandoned one of the key theses
of *A People Highly Favoured of God*. Nothing could have been further from
the truth, for my scholarly attachment to the so-called "Stewart-Rawlyk"
thesis remained strong. In my view, many Nova Scotians were certainly
disoriented by the often conflicting forces unleashed by the American
Revolution, and the powerful "Sense of Mission" theme articulated by
Alline helped them deal with their collective "Confusion, Trouble and
Anguish."[16] Yet there was also a spiritual and religious dimension to their
reaction as well — a dimension which Goldwin French in his perceptive
review of *A People Highly Favoured of God* felt Gordon Stewart and I had
not adequately dealt with.[17]

What seemed to help me to respond positively to the French critique, almost a decade after it had been made, were the insights I had received from my reading of Wallace and Turner, in particular. These two social anthropologists gave me a certain degree of academic respectability and encouragement at a time when I had serious reservations about being too sympathetic or showing too much empathy for the Canadian evangelical tradition. I felt a deep inner need in 1982 and 1983, in particular, to re-examine the Nova Scotia revivalist tradition in general and Henry Alline in particular. But I did not want to jettison whatever academic reputation I had by being too closely associated with revivals and revivalists — even in the distant Canadian past. From my vantage point at Queen's University, I understood only too well the secular bias of so much Canadian historical writing, and I did not want to be pushed even further to the outer margins of the profession. My work on the Maritimes had already done this, to a certain degree, I was sure, since for so many Canadian historians Maritime historians are of peripheral importance, cut off as they are from the Central Canada and the Western cutting edge of the discipline. To underscore this further, for many, the marginality of my work was the fact that so much of it dealt with the seventeenth and eighteenth centuries — the so-called Dark Ages of Canadian history. If they did not happen after 1867, Canadian events, according to the standard version of Canadian historical writing, were and are of little lasting consequence or importance. Thus my regional emphasis and my research time-frame had already pushed me out of the mainstream of Canadian historiography. Writing about revivals and revivalists would, I was certain, push me even further to the outskirts. However, it was clear to me as early as October 1981, when I was asked by Acadia Divinity College to give the 1983 Hayward Lectures, that I had less and less to lose in so doing. And there was perhaps something to gain. I could at least be involved in a vigorous North American debate about the evangelical tradition. I had realized by the mid-1970s that even though many Canadian scholars were not very interested in my work about New England–Nova Scotia relations in the seventeenth and eighteenth centuries, some American scholars definitely were. And furthermore, I knew from reviews, letters and invitations that a number of American religious scholars were, in fact, taking some of my work on Maritime religion very seriously indeed. I saw this first in Stephen Marini's "New England Folk Religions 1770-1815: The Sectarian Impulse in Revolutionary Society" (Ph.D. Harvard University, 1978) later published by Harvard University Press under the title *Radical Sects of Revolutionary New England* (Cambridge, 1982). Then I saw it in

not lose sight of the premise that, just as in the Incarnation Christ's humanity does not compromise his divinity so the reality of God's other work in history, going well beyond what we might explain as natural phenomena, is not compromised by the fact that it is culturally defined.

Then Marsden goes on:

The history of Christianity reveals a perplexing mixture of divine and human factors. As Richard Lovelace has said, this history, when viewed without a proper awareness of the spiritual forces involved, "is as confusing as a football game in which half the players are invisible." The present work, an analysis of cultural influences on religious belief, is a study of things visible. As such it must necessarily reflect more than a little sympathy with the modern mode of explanation in terms of natural historical causation. Yet it would be a mistake to assume that such sympathy is incompatible with, or even antagonistic to, a view of history in which God as revealed in Scripture is the dominant force, and in which other unseen spiritual forces are contending. I find that a Christian view of history is clarified if one considers reality as more or less like the world portrayed in the works of J. R. R. Tolkien. We live in the midst of contests between great and mysterious spiritual forces, which we understand only imperfectly and whose true dimensions we only occasionally glimpse. Yet, frail as we are, we do play a role in this history, on the side either of the powers of light or of the powers of darkness. It is crucially important then, that, by God's grace, we keep our wits about us and discern the vast difference between the real forces for good and the powers of darkness disguised as angels of light.[19]

As far as Marsden is concerned, the "Christian historian," though attached to certain theological criteria, may nevertheless "refrain from explicit judgments on what is properly Christian" while at the same time concentrating "on observable cultural forces." "By identifying these forces," he or she "provides material which individuals of various theological persuasions may use to help distinguish God's genuine work from practices that have no greater authority than the customs or ways of thinking of a particular time and place."[20]

Though I may have some serious intellectual reservations about the

Lovelace-Tolkien-Marsden view of cosmic reality, I see in it as plausible an explanatory device for historical development and change as many widely used and academically popular theories. Though this view may not influence directly my own historical approach, it nevertheless has compelled me to look at a possible empathetic approach to the evangelical tradition in a far more sympathetic manner. If neo-Marxists can write neo-Marxist history, why should not evangelical Christian historians — like Marsden — write from an evangelical Christian perspective? And, furthermore, why should not a scholar knowledgeable and at least sympathetic to the evangelical tradition today write about the evangelical tradition of yesterday? There is no reason for me to make pious and "explicit judgments on what is properly Christian." It is my hope, as it is Marsden's, that by identifying some of "these observable cultural forces," I will help people whose theological views are quite different from mine to "distinguish God's genuine work from practices that have no greater authority than the customs or ways of thinking of a particular time and place." At one time such an approach would have been anathema to me. Today it is not. And for this fundamental change of perspective I am grateful to scholars like George Marsden.

CANADA — CHART 1

	Population	No Religion	Church of England
1911	7,206,643	26,027 (0.3)*	1,043,017 (14.4)
1921	8,788,483	n/a	1,407,994 (16.0)
1931	10,376,786	21,071 (0.2)	1,635,615 (15.70
1941	11,506,655	2,326 (0)	1,751,168 (15.2)
1951	14,009,429	59,679 (0.4)	2,060,720 (14.7)
1961	18,238,247	n/a	2,409,068 (13.2)
1971	21,568,310	929,580 (4.3)	2,543,175 (11.8)
1981	24,083,495	1,752,380 (7.2)	2,436,375 (10.1)

	Methodist	Salvation Army	Pentecostal
1911	1,079,892 (15.0)	18,834 (0.2)	513 (0)
1921	1,159,458 (13.2)	24,733 (0.2)	n/a
1931	7,730 (0)	30,716 (0.3)	26,301 (0.2)
1941	8,788 (0)	33,548 (0.3)	57,646 (0.5)
1951	8,921 (0)	70,275 (0.5)	95,131 (0.6)
1961	n/a	n/a	143,877 (0.7)
1971	19,125 (0.1)	119,665 (0.5)	220,390 (1.0)

	Presbyterian	Roman Catholic
1911	1,115,324 (15.4)	2,833,041 (39.3)
1921	1,409,407 (16.0)	3,389,636 (38.5)
1931	870,728 (8.4)	4.295.399)41/3
1941	829,147 (7.2)	4,800,895 (41.7)
1951	781,747 (5.5)	6,069,496 (43.3)
1961	818,558 (4.4)	8,342,826 (43.7)
1971	872,330 (4.0)	9,974,895 (46.2)
1981	812,105 (3.3)	11,210,390 (46.5)

*The figures which appear in brackets represent the percentage of the country total population.

	Baptist	United Church
1911	382,660 (5.3)	n/a
1921	421,731 (4.8)	n/a
1931	443,341 (4.2)	2,017,375 (19.4)
1941	483,592 (4.2)	2,204,875 (19.1)
1951	519,585 (3.7)	2,867,271 (20.4)
1961	593,553 (3.2)	3,664,008 (20.1)
1971	667,245 (3.1)	3,768,805 (17.4)
1981	696,850 (2.9)	3,758,015 (15.6)

BRITISH COLUMBIA — CHART 2

	Population	No Religion	Church of England
1911	392,480	7,007 (1.7)*	100,952 (25.7)
1921	524,582	n/a	160,978 (30.6)
1931	694,263	7,855 (1.1)	205,047 (29.5)
1941	817,861	226 (0)	245,531 (30.0)
1951	1,165,210	25,396 (2.1)	315,469 (27.0)
1961	1,629,082	n/a	367,096 (22.5)
1971	2,184,620	287,115 (13.1)	386,670 (17.7)
1981	2,713,615	556,180 (20.5)	374,055 (13.7)

	Methodist	Salvation Army	Pentecostal
1911	52,132 (13.2)	1,842 (0.4)	2 (0)
1921	64,810 (12.3)	2,086 (0.4)	n/a
1931	140 (0)	2,801 (0.4)	2,277 (0.3)
1941	391 (0)	3,880 (0.4)	5,235 (0.6)
1951	409 (0)	4,945 (0.4)	11,781 (1.0)
1961	n/a	n/a	19,998 (1.2)
1971	1,860 (0)	11,885 (0.5)	35,225 (1.6)
1981	6,340 (0.2)	12,270 (0.4)	55,095 (2.0)

	Presbyterian	Roman Catholic
1911	82,125 (20.9)	58,397 (14.8)
1921	123,022 (23.4)	63,980 (12.1)
1931	84,183 (12.1)	90,852 (13.0)
1941	94,300 (11.5)	109,634 (13.4)
1951	97,151 (8.3)	168,016 (14.4)
1961	90,093 (5.5)	285,184 (17.5)
1971	100,940 (4.6)	408,330 (18.7)
1981	89,810 (3.3)	526,355 (19.4)

*The figures which appear in brackets represent the percentage of the province's total population.

	Baptist	United Church
1911	17,228 (4.3)	n/a
1921	20,158 (3.8)	n/a
1931	23,395 (3.3)	164,750 (23.7)
1941	29,780 (3.6)	200,817 (24.5)
1951	39,445 (3.3)	341,914 (29.3)
1961	49,481 (3.0)	504,317 (30.9)
1971	64,835 (2.9)	537,565 (24.6)
1981	81,850 (3.0)	548,360 (20.2)

ENDNOTES
INTRODUCTION

1. See, for example, the emphasis placed upon "social relevance" in the evalua-
tion of applications for Canada Council and SSHRCC research grants. N.
Jackson of the Canada Council Killam Research Fellowship Programme to
G. A. Rawlyk, August 4, 1987 (letter in possession of the author).
2. See S. A. Marini, "New England Folk Religions 1770-1815: The Sectarian
Impulse in Revolutionary Society" (Ph.D. dissertation, Harvard University,
1978), p. 20.
3. Letter from H. H. Budd to Robert Wright, April 1986 (letter in possession of
Robert Wright, Millbrook, Ont.).
4. See the important study by J. G. Stackhouse, Jr., "Proclaiming the Word:
Canadian Evangelicalism Since World War I" (Ph.D. dissertation, University
of Chicago, 1987).
5. See David Weale, "The Ministry of the Reverend Donald McDonald on
Prince Edward Island 1826-1867: A Case Study Examination of the Influence
and Role of Religion within Colonial Society" (Ph.D. dissertation, Queen's
University, 1976), pp. 107-116.
6. See G. A. Rawlyk, *New Light Letters and Songs* (Hantsport, N.S., 1983).

CHAPTER I

1. This chapter is a much-revised version of part of my "Historical Background"
chapter in *New Light Letters and Songs*, pp. 4-22. For a discussion of the
"neutrality" thesis see M. Armstrong, "Neutrality and Religion in Revolutionary Nova Scotia," *The New England Quarterly*, IX (March 1940), pp. 50-62.
2. See, in particular, J. M. Bumsted, *Henry Alline* (Toronto, 1971), p. 78 and D.
G. Bell, ed., *Newlight Baptist Journals of James Manning and James Innis*
(Hantsport, N.S., 1984), p. xiii.
3. Gordon Stewart and G. A. Rawlyk, *A People Highly Favoured of God*
(Toronto, 1972).
4. J. More, *The History of Queens County Nova Scotia* (Halifax, 1873), p. 162.
5. See J. Davis, *Life and Times of the Late Rev. Harris Harding, Yarmouth, N.S.*
(Charlottetown, P.E.I., 1866), p. 178.
6. William James, *Varieties of Religious Experience* (New York, 1902), pp. 159,
217.
7. M. E. Marty, *Modern American Religion: The Irony of It All 1893-1919*, Vol. I
(Chicago, 1986), p. 42.
8. H. Alline, *Life and Journal* (Boston, 1806), pp. 26-27.
9. Ibid., pp. 27, 34.
10. Ibid., pp. 34-35.
11. Ibid., p. 35.

12. The central importance of the "New Birth" in the New Light experience in New England's "First Great Awakening" is discussed in A. Heimert, *Religion and the American Mind from the Great Awakening to the Revolution* (Cambridge, Mass., 1966).

13. For a more detailed discussion of Alline's theology, see G. A. Rawlyk, *Henry Alline: Selected Writings* (New York, 1987), pp. 17-29.

14. H. Alline, *The Anti-Traditionalist* (Halifax, 1783), pp. 24-25.

15. Ibid., p. 40.

16. Ibid., pp. 62-63.

17. H. Alline, *Two Mites on Some of the Most Important and Much Disputed Points of Divinity* (Halifax, 1781), pp. 20-21.

18. Alline, *The Anti-Traditionalist*, p. 65.

19. See Alline, *Two Mites*, pp. 121-135.

20. Ibid., pp. 124-125.

21. Ibid., p. 126.

22. Quoted in a letter fragment in the Manning Papers, Acadia University Archives, Wolfville, Nova Scotia (subsequently referred to as A.U.A.).

23. Alline, *Two Mites*, pp. 128-129.

24. Ibid., pp. 132-133.

25. Ibid., pp. 150-151.

26. Alline, *The Anti-Traditionalist*, pp. 53-54.

27. Marini, "New England Folk Religions," p. 2. See Marini's *Radical Sects of Revolutionary New England* (Cambridge, Ma., 1982) for an excellent discussion of Alline's impact on northern New England.

28. M. Richey, *A Memoir of the Late Rev. William Black* (Halifax, 1839), p. 45.

29. Quoted in Marini, "New England Folk Religions," pp. 453-454.

30. Ibid., p. 479.

31. This theme is developed in D. D. Bruce, Jr., *And They All Sang Hallelujah, Plain-Folk Camp Meeting Religion 1800-1845* (Knoxville, Tenn., 1975), p. 95. See also Marini, *Radical Sects*, pp. 156-171, and the soon-to-be-published (by Yale University Press) *The Democratization of American Christianity* by Nathan O. Hatch.

32. For a far more critical assessment of these hymns, see M. Armstrong, "Henry Alline's Spiritual Hymns and Songs," *Dalhousie Review*, Vol. XXXIV (1954-5), pp. 418-425. The best treatment of Alline's *Hymns and Spiritual Songs* is to be found in M. Filschie, " 'Redeeming Love Shall Be Our Song': Hymns of the First Great Awakening in Nova Scotia" (M.A. dissertation, Queen's University, 1983).

33. H. Alline, *Hymns and Spiritual Songs on a Variety of Pleasing and Important Subjects* (Boston, 1786), pp. i-ii.

34. Ibid., pp. 51-52.

35. Ibid., p. 131.

36. Ibid., pp. 153-154.

37. Ibid., p. 162.

38. Ibid., pp. 182-183.

39. Ibid., pp. 348-349.

40. Ibid., pp. 380-381.

41. I have attended one of these services and I found it, without question, memorable. This service convinced me that I had, in my earlier work on Alline, significantly underestimated the powerful impact that the Allinite oral tradition had on Maritime religious culture in the nineteenth *and* twentieth centuries.

42. M. Armstrong, *The Great Awakening in Nova Scotia 1776-1809* (Hartford, Conn., 1948), p. 92.
43. See G. Patterson, *Memoir of the Rev. James McGregor* (Philadelphia, 1859), p. 92.
44. Armstrong, *The Great Awakening*, p. 92.
45. See Gordon Stewart's Ph.D. dissertation, "Religion and the Yankee Mind of Nova Scotia During the American Revolution" (Queen's University, 1971). This dissertation, in a much-revised form, was published the following year under the title *A People Highly Favoured of God.*
46. Armstrong, *The Great Awakening in Nova Scotia*, p. 86. On Alline's New Hampshire tombstone the following sentence was added to the original inscription: "He was a burning and a shining light and justly esteemed the Apostle of Nova Scotia."
47. D. C. Harvey and C. B. Fergusson, eds., *The Diary of Simeon Perkins, 1780-1780*, Vol. II (Toronto, 1958), p. 169.
48. Ibid., p. 168.
49. Ibid., p. 172.
50. Ibid., p. 174.
51. Ibid., p. 169.
52. Ibid.
53. J. Beverley and B. Moody, eds., *The Life and Journal of The Rev. Mr. Henry Alline* (Hantsport, N.S., 1982), pp. 208-209.
54. Ibid., p. 210.
55. Ibid.
56. Harvey and Fergusson, *The Diary of Simeon Perkins*, p. 177.
57. Ibid.
58. "Records of the Church of Jebogue in Yarmouth," Public Archives of Nova Scotia, p. 140 (subsequently referred to as P.A.N.S.).
59. Heimert, *Religion and the American Mind*, p. 169.
60. Beverley and Moody, *The Journal of Henry Alline*, p. 210.
61. Davis, *Harding*, p. 187.
62. Ibid.
63. Mary Coy Bradley, *Life and Christian Experiences* (Boston, 1849), p. 16.
64. Ibid.
65. Patterson Scrapbook, H. Chipman to Messrs. Cock and Smith, June 30, 1777, P.A.N.S.
66. For a further discussion of this theme, see Rawlyk, *Ravished by the Spirit*, pp. 73-136.
67. Beverley and Moody, *The Journal of Henry Alline*, p. 63.
68. Ibid., pp. 60-64.
69. Alline, *Two Mites*, pp. 150-151.
70. Armstrong, *The Great Awakening in Nova Scotia*, pp. 95-96.
71. H. Adams, *Alphabetical Compendium of the Various Sects which have Appeared in the World* (Boston, 1784), pp. lxiv-lxv.
72. Alline, *The Anti-Traditionalist*, pp. 24-25.
73. Armstrong, *The Great Awakening in Nova Scotia*, p. 97.
74. Alline, *The Anti-Traditionalist*, p. 31.
75. Beverley and Moody, *The Journal of Henry Alline*, p. 63.
76. Alline, *Two Mites*, p. 94.
77. Alline, *The Anti-Traditionalist*, p. 40.
78. Alline, *Two Mites*, p. 95.
79. Armstrong, *The Great Awakening in Nova Scotia*, p. 101.

80. Alline, *Two Mites*, p. 93.
81. Alline, *The Anti-Traditionalist*, p. 42.
82. Beverley and Moody, *The Journal of Henry Alline*, p. 216.
83. This is the essential thesis of Marini's *Radical Sects of Revolutionary New England.*
84. J. Scott, *A Brief View of the Religious Tenets and Sentiments of Mr. Henry Alline* (Halifax, 1784), pp. 255-257.
85. Quoted in Rawlyk, *New Light Letters and Songs*, p. 218.
86. Armstrong, *The Great Awakening in Nova Scotia*, p. 105.
87. See Scott's preoccupation with this problem in his *Brief View*, pp. 255-257.
88. Ibid., pp. 169-189.
89. Ibid., p. 188.
90. See Gordon Stewart's important article "Charisma and Integration: an Eighteenth Century North American Case," *Comparative Studies in Society and History*, XVI (1974), pp. 138-149.
91. Beverley and Moody, *The Journal of Henry Alline*, pp. 60-66.
92. H. Alline, *A Gospel Call to Sinners* (Newburyport, Mass., 1795), p. 29.
93. Edward Manning's "Reminiscences" in the Manning Papers, A.U.A.
94. Armstrong, *The Great Awakening in Nova Scotia*, p. 105.
95. See Rawlyk, *Ravished by the Spirit*, pp. 74-104.
96. Ibid., p. 174.
97. Bell, *Newlight Baptist Journals*, pp. 22-35.
98. Quoted in J. B. Bowles, *The Great Revival 1787-1805: The Origins of the Southern Evangelical Mind* (Lexington, Ky., 1972), p. 112.
99. Bell, *Newlight Baptist Journals*, p. xiii.

CHAPTER II

1. Alline, *Life and Journal*, pp. 38-39. This chapter is a much-revised version of Chapter I of *Ravished by the Spirit*, pp. 17-35.
2. Alline, *Life and Journal*, pp. 39-41.
3. Ibid., pp. 41-42.
4. Ibid., pp. 42-43.
5. Ibid., p. 44.
6. Ibid.
7. Ibid., pp. 46-48.
8. Ibid., p. 47.
9. Ibid., p. 48.
10. Ibid., p. 54.
11. Ibid., pp. 56-57.
12. Ibid., p. 59.
13. Ibid., pp. 61-62.
14. Ibid., p. 68.
15. Ibid., p. 70.
16. Ibid., pp. 71-73.
17. Ibid., pp. 73-74.
18. Ibid., pp. 75-78.
19. Ibid., pp. 78-82.
20. Ibid., pp. 82-89.
21. Ibid., p. 85.
22. Ibid., p. 93.
23. Ibid., p. 103.

24. Ibid., pp. 105-136.
25. Peter Shaw, *American Patriots and the Rituals of Revolution* (Cambridge, Mass., 1981), p. 165.
26. Alline, *Life and Journal*, p. 131.
27. Ibid., pp. 131-133.
28. Ibid., p. 136.
29. Ibid., p. 140.
30. Ibid., p. 143.
31. Ibid.
32. Ibid., p. 144.
33. Ibid.
34. Ibid., p. 145.
35. Ibid., pp. 146-149.
36. Ibid., pp. 149-153.
37. Ibid., pp. 153-164.
38. Ibid., pp. 165-167.
39. Ibid., pp. 168-170.
40. Ibid., p. 171.
41. Ibid., pp. 172-173.
42. Hannah Adams, *Alphabetical Compendium of the Various Sects* (Boston, 1784), pp. lxiv-lxv.
43. Adams, *Compendium*, p. lxv.
44. Alline, *Life and Journal*, p. 180; David McLure to William Alline, August 3, 1784.
45. Ibid.
46. "North Hampton Congregational Church Book," New Hampshire Historical Society, Concord, N.H.
47. See, for example, "Henry Alline" in the *Christian Instructor and Missionary Register of the Presbyterian Church of Nova Scotia* (March 1859), p. 74.
48. Quoted in Armstrong, *The Great Awakening in Nova Scotia*, p. 86.
49. See the "Records of the Church of Jebogue in Yarmouth," p. 138 in the P.A.N.S.
50. Harvey and Fergusson, *The Diary of Simeon Perkins 1780-1789*, p. 177.
51. See, for example, Alline, *The Anti-Traditionalist*, p. 36.
52. H. Alline, *A Sermon Preached at Liverpool, 20 November, 1782* (Halifax, N.S.), p. 23.
53. Alline, *The Anti-Traditionalist*, p. 24.
54. Ibid., p. 48. See also the many hymns written by Alline which stressed the "ravishing process."
55. Donald Mathews, *Religion in the Old South* (Chicago, 1977), pp. 105-110.
56. Mary P. Ryan, "A Women's Awakening: Evangelical Religion and the Families of Utica, New York, 1800-1840," in J. W. James, ed., *Women in American Religion* (Philadelphia, 1980), p. 110.
57. Ibid.
58. Mathews, *Religion in the Old South*, p. 110.
59. Alline, *Two Mites*, p. 234.
60. G. A. Rawlyk, "Henry Alline and the Canadian Baptist Tradition," *McMaster Divinity College Theological Bulletin*, Vol. IV, No. 4 (June 1977), p. 6.
61. See E. L. Tuveson, *Redeemer Nation: The Idea of America's Millennial Role* (Chicago 1968).

CHAPTER III

1. For a more detailed discussion of this antinomian movement see Bell, *New-light Journals*, and Rawlyk, *Ravished by the Spirit*.
2. This chapter is a much-revised version of a paper originally given at Asbury Theological Seminary, Wilmore, Kentucky, in July 1986.
3. See T. W. Smith, *History of the Methodist church... of Eastern British North America* (Halifax, 1877), pp. 150-151; G. French, *Parsons and Politics* (Toronto, 1962), pp. 33-39; N. Bangs, *The Life of the Rev. Freeborn Garrettson* (New York, 1830), pp. 150-158; W. C. Barclay, *Early American Methodism 1769-1844*, Vol. I (New York, 1949), pp. 166-171; N. A. McNairn, "Mission in Nova Scotia," *Methodist History*, Vol. 12 (Jan. 1974), pp. 3-18; R. D. Simpson, "Freeborn Garrettson: American Methodist Pioneer" (Ph.D. dissertation, Drew Theological Seminary, 1954); R. D. Simpson, ed., *American Methodist Pioneer: The Life and Journals of the Rev. Freeborn Garrettson 1752-1827* (Rutland, Vt., 1984); G. A. Rawlyk, "Freeborn Garrettson," *Dictionary of Canadian Biography 1821-1835*, Vol. VI (Toronto, 1987), pp. 275-276.
4. See N. MacKinnon, *This Unfriendly Soil: The Loyalist Experience in Nova Scotia 1783-1791* (Montreal, 1985).
5. Gordon Wood, "Evangelical America and Early Mormonism" (paper presented to the 15th annual meeting of the Mormon History Association, May 1980), p. 2. See also Nathan Hatch's soon-to-be-published volume, *The Democratization of American Christianity* (New Haven, Conn. 1989).
6. J. M. Cramp's "History of the Maritime Baptists," A.U.A.
7. Wood, "Evangelical America," p. 7. See also Hatch, *The Democratization of American Christianity*, especially Chapter I, "American Christianity in an Age of Democratic Revolution," and Chapter II, "The Crisis of Authority in Popular Culture."
8. Wood, "Evangelical America," p. 10.
9. Wood, "Evangelical America," p. 12.
10. See Rawlyk, *New Light Letters and Songs*, pp. 37-63.
11. Barclay, *Early American Methodism*, Vol. I (New York, 1949) p. 171.
12. J. M. Buckley, *A History of Methodism in the United States*, Vol. 1 (New York, 1897), p. 369.
13. Quoted in Smith, *History of the Methodist Church*, pp. 193-194.
14. Quoted in Bangs, *Garrettson*, p. 154.
15. Buckley, *A History of Methodism*, p. 171.
16. Rawlyk, "Freeborn Garrettson," p. 275.
17. Quoted in Smith, *History of the Methodist Church*, p. 152.
18. Ibid.
19. Quoted in Rawlyk, "Freeborn Garrettson," p. 275.
20. Quoted in Bangs, *Garrettson*, p. 177.
21. Ibid., p. 172.
22. *Methodist Magazine* (1827), p. 272.
23. W. H. Williams, *The Garden of American Methodism: The Delmarva Peninsula 1769-1820* (Wilmington, Del., 1984), p. 32.
24. Ibid.
25. Ibid.
26. Quoted in Williams, *The Garden of Methodism*, p. 32.
27. "Freeborn Garrettson Journal," United Church Archives, Toronto (subsequently referred to as U.C.A.).

28. Ibid.
29. Ibid.
30. Simpson, *American Methodist Pioneer: The Life and Journals of the Rev. Freeborn Garrettson*, p. 127.
31. Quoted in Smith, *History of the Methodist Church*, p. 166.
32. "Freeborn Garrettson Journal," U.C.A.
33. Ibid.
34. Simpson, *American Methodist Pioneer: The Life and Journals of the Rev. Freeborn Garrettson*, pp. 129-130.
35. Quoted in Bangs, *Garrettson*, p. 171.
36. Simpson, *American Methodist Pioneer: The Life and Journals of the Rev. Freeborn Garrettson*, p. 131.
37. Quoted in Barclay, *Early American Methodism*, Vol. I, p. 171.
38. See Rawlyk, "Freeborn Garrettson," p. 276.
39. See Smith, *History of the Methodist Church*, pp. 200-209.
40. Ibid., p. 197.
41. Ibid., p. 99. See also Simpson, *American Methodist Pioneer: The Life and Journals of the Rev. Freeborn Garrettson*, p. 131.
42. This material is taken from David Stratas, "A Study of the Historical Demography of the Maritime Provinces 1763-1901" (unpublished paper, Dept. of History, Queen's University, August 1981).
43. Barry Moody, "From Itinerant to Pastor: the Case of Edward Manning (1767-1851)," *Papers of the Canadian Society of Church History* (1981), pp. 1-25.
44. Cramp, "History of the Maritime Baptists," A.U.A.
45. Ibid.
46. Ibid.
47. Ibid. See also G. E. Levy, ed., *The Diary of Joseph Dimock* (Hantsport, 1979).
48. I. E. Bill, *Fifty Years with the Baptist Ministers and Churches of the Maritime Provinces of Canada* (Saint John, N.B., 1880), p. 201.
49. Ibid., pp. 201-202.
50. E. M. Saunders, *History of the Baptists of the Maritime Provinces* (Halifax, 1902), p. 93.
51. Harvey and Fergusson, *The Diary of Simeon Perkins 1790-1796*, p. 177.
52. Harvey and Fergusson, *The Diary of Simeon Perkins 1797-1803*, p. 18.
53. Harvey and Fergusson, *The Diary of Simeon Perkins 1790-1796*, p. 428.
54. Davis, *Harding*, p. 26.
55. Ibid., pp. 146-148.
56. Quoted in Davis, *Harding*, p. 168.
57. Quoted in Davis, *Harding*, p. 153.
58. Quoted in Davis, *Harding*, p. 143.
59. Davis, *Harding*, pp. 7-8.
60. Ibid., p. 7.
61. Quoted in Davis, *Harding*, p. 10.
62. Davis, *Harding*, p. 178.
63. See Rawlyk, *Henry Alline*, pp. 5-17.
64. Cramp, "History of the Maritime Baptists," A.U.A.
65. Quoted in Davis, *Harding*, p. 206.
66. Quoted in Bill, *Fifty Years*, p. 142.
67. Saunders, *History of the Baptists*, p. 311.
68. Quoted in Saunders, *History of the Baptists*, p. 311.
69. Bill, *Fifty Years*, p. 143.

70. Ibid., pp. 151-152.
71. Moody, "From Itinerant to Settled Pastor," pp. 1-25.
72. "Reminiscences," Manning Papers, A.U.A.
73. Rawlyk, *Ravished by the Spirit*, pp. 81-85.
74. See MacKinnon, *This Unfriendly Soil*.
75. Quoted in French, *Parsons and Politics*, p. 34.
76. Quoted in French, *Parsons and Politics*, p. 35.
77. French, *Parsons and Politics*, p. 35.
78. Ibid., p. 36.
79. Ibid., p. 38.
80. Ibid., p. 65.
81. Quoted in French, *Parsons and Politics*, p. 65.
82. Simpson, *American Methodist Pioneer: The Life and Journals of the Rev. Freeborn Garrettson*, p. 6.
83. McNairn, "Mission to Nova Scotia," pp. 3-18.

CHAPTER IV

1. J. Davis, *Life and Times of Harris Harding*, p. 75. This chapter is a revised version of my "From Newlight to Baptist: Harris Harding and the Second Great Awakening in Nova Scotia" in B. Moody, ed., *Repent and Believe* (Hantsport, N.S., 1980), pp. 1-26, 151-100.
2. W. G. McLoughlin, *Revivals, Awakenings and Reform* (Chicago, 1978), pp. 1-23.
3. See R. D. Shiels, "The Myth of the Second Great Awakening" (paper delivered at the American Historical Association, Dec. 28, 1977); R. Birdsall, "The Second Great Awakening and the New England Social Order," *Church History*, 39 (1970), pp. 345-364; McLoughlin, *Revivals, Awakenings and Reforms*, pp. 98-140; W. R. Cross, *The Burned-Over District: The Social and Intellectual History of Enthusiastic Religion in Western New York 1800-1850* (Ithaca, 1950); R. Carwardine, "The Second Great Awakening in the Urban Centers: A Examination of Methodism and the 'New Measures,'" *Journal of American History*, 59 (1972), pp. 338-350; Johnson, *A Shopkeeper's Millennium*; T. D. Bilhartz, *Urban Religion and the Second Great Awakening: Church and Society in Early National Baltimore* (Rutherford, N.J., 1986); R. Carwardine, *Transatlantic Revivalism: Popular Evangelicalism in Britain and America 1790-1865* (Westport, 1978). For the best treatment of the role of evangelical religion in the "Early Republic" see N. O. Hatch, *The Democratization of American Christianity* (New Haven, 1989). For the Nova Scotia side of the Second Great Awakening story see Armstrong, *The Great Awakening*; Clark, *Church and Sect*; and Rawlyk, *Ravished by the Spirit*. An often overlooked yet important study is G. E. Levy, *The Baptists of the Maritime Provinces 1753-1946* (Saint John, N.B., 1946), especially pp. 41-85.
4. M. Armstrong, "Neutrality and Religion in Revolutionary Nova Scotia" in G. A. Rawlyk, ed., *Historical Essays on the Atlantic Provinces* (Toronto, 1967), p. 40.
5. S. D. Clark, *Movements of Political Protest in Canada 1640-1840* (Toronto, 1959), p. 7.
6. Bumsted, *Henry Alline*, p. 68.
7. See Stewart and Rawlyk, *A People Highly Favoured of God*.
8. See Rawlyk, *Ravished by the Spirit*.
9. *Massachusetts Baptist Missionary Magazine* (1808), pp. 303-305.

10. Ibid., pp. 305-307.
11. Ibid.
12. Ibid., p. 307.
13. Ibid., pp. 307-309.
14. Ibid.
15. See "The Journal of Mr. Reverend John Payzant . . . 1790-1810," P.A.N.S. See also B. Cuthbertson, ed., *The Journal of the Reverend John Payzant (1749-1834)*, (Hantsport, N.S., 1981).
16. "Payzant Journal," P.A.N.S.
17. G. E. Levy, ed., *The Diary of Joseph Dimock* (Hantsport, N.S., 1979), pp. 83-84.
18. Davis, *Harding*, p. 168.
19. Rawlyk, *Ravished by the Spirit*, pp. 112-118.
20. "Payzant Journal," P.A.N.S.
21. Davis, *Harding*, pp. 21-40.
22. Ibid., p. 143.
23. Ibid.
24. Fergusson, *The Diary of Simeon Perkins 1790-1796*, p. 174.
25. Davis, *Harding*, p. 33.
26. See Rawlyk, *New Light Letters and Songs*, pp. 91-176.
27. Quoted in Davis, *Harding*, p. 224.
28. Harding to John Payzant, Aug. 23, 1791; quoted in Rawlyk, *New Light Letters and Songs*, p. 133.
29. Harding to Thomas Bennett, April 21, 1792; quoted in Rawlyk, *New Light Letters and Songs*, p. 166.
30. Ibid., p. 136.
31. Harding to Dorcas Prentice, Aug. 27, 1791; in Rawlyk, *New Light Letters and Songs*, p. 147.
32. Harding to Dorcas Prentice, Sept. 17, 1791; in Rawlyk, *New Light Letters and Songs*, p. 158.
33. Harding to W. Alline, April 6, 1792; in Cramp, "History of the Maritime Baptists," A.U.A.
34. Harding to Dorcas Prentice, Aug. 21, 1791; in Rawlyk, *New Light Letters and Songs*, p. 147.
35. Cramp, "History of the Maritime Baptists," A.U.A.
36. See Rawlyk, *Ravished by the Spirit*, pp. 81-85.
37. Quoted in Cramp, "History of the Maritime Baptists," A.U.A.
38. See "Payzant Journal," P.A.N.S.
39. Ibid.
40. Fergusson, *Diary of Simeon Perkins 1797-1803*, p. 45.
41. Levy, *Diary of Joseph Dimock*, p. 13.
42. Cramp, "History of the Maritime Baptists," A.U.A.
43. "Payzant Journal," P.A.N.S.
44. Levy, *Baptists of the Maritime Provinces*, p. 52.
45. Cramp, "History of the Maritime Baptists," P.A.N.S.
46. Saunders, *History of the Baptists*, p. 28.
47. Ibid., p. 71.
48. Quoted in Cramp, "History of the Maritime Baptists," P.A.N.S.
49. Harding, "Account of the Rise and Progress of the First Baptist Church in Yarmouth"; quoted in Davis, *Harding*, p. 206.
50. "Chebogue Church Records," P.A.N.S. See also H. E. Scott, Jr., ed., *The Journal of the Reverend Jonathan Scott* (Boston, 1980).

51. See Harding to Dimock, Jan. 27, 1792; in Rawlyk, *New Light Letters and Songs*, p. 161; and Harding to Bennett, April 6, 1792, in Rawlyk, *New Light Letters and Songs*, pp. 163-164.
52. Quoted in Cramp, "History of the Maritime Baptists," A.U.A.
53. Fergusson, *Diary of Simeon Perkins 1790-1796*, p. 386.
54. Ibid., p. 387.
55. Mrs. S. Wright to T. Bennett, Sept. 26, 1793; in Rawlyk, *New Light Letters and Songs*, p. 178.
56. "Payzant Journal," P.A.N.S.
57. Ibid.
58. Fergusson, *Diary of Simeon Perkins 1797-1803*, p. 26.
59. Davis, *Harding*, p. 73.
60. Cramp, "History of the Maritime Baptists," A.U.A.
61. Quoted in "History of the Maritime Baptists," A.U.A.
62. *Classified Digest of the Records of the Society for the Propagation of the Gospel in Foreign Parts 1701-1892* (London, 1893), p. 118.
63. Quoted in Saunders, *History of the Baptists*, p. 115.
64. Ibid.
65. Cramp, "History of the Maritime Baptists," P.A.N.S.
66. Quoted in Cramp, "History of the Maritime Baptists," P.A.N.S.
67. Ibid.
68. "Payzant Journal," P.A.N.S.
69. Ibid.
70. Quoted in Cramp, "History of the Maritime Baptists," A.U.A.
71. Ibid.
72. Quoted in Cramp, "History of the Maritime Baptists," A.U.A.
73. Quoted in Cramp, "History of the Maritime Baptists," A.U.A.
74. J. Fingard, *The Anglican Design in Loyalist Nova Scotia 1783-1816* (London, 1792), p. 60.
75. Quoted in Davis, *Harding*, p. 79.
76. Ibid., p. 23.
77. P. Miller, *Errand Into The Wilderness* (Cambridge, Mass., 1964), p. 167.
78. Davis, *Harding*, p. 220.
79. Ibid.
80. Ibid., pp. 217-218.
81. See W. J. Ong, *The Presence of the Word: Some Prolegomena for Cultural and Religious History* (New Haven, Conn., 1967).
82. Davis, *Harding*, p. 101.
83. Ibid., pp. 102-103.
84. Quoted in Cramp, "History of the Maritime Baptists," A.U.A.
85. Ibid.
86. Ibid.
87. Ibid.
88. Ibid.
89. Davis, *Harding*, p. 149.
90. Ibid., p. 136.
91. Ibid., pp. 136-137.
92. See how this thesis regarding applying one "Awakening" paradigm to another is developed in R. D. Shiels, "The Connecticut Clergy in the Second Great Awakening" (Ph.D. dissertation, Boston University, 1976).

93. For a somewhat different view of Harding in the early nineteenth century, see D. C. Goodwin's M.A. dissertation, "Advancing Light: Evangelicalism in Yarmouth Township, 1761-1830."

CHAPTER V

1. R. N. Bellah, et. al., *Habits of the Heart: Individualism and Commitment in American Life* (Berkeley, 1985). This is a much-revised version of a paper first delivered at the Kingston Historical Society on Feb. 25, 1987.
2. See B. Palmer, *A Culture in Conflict* (Montreal, 1978), p. 239.
3. Bellah, *Habits of the Heart*, p. 83.
4. See S. Toulmin, *The Return To Cosmology: Postmodern Science and the Theology of Nature* (Berkeley, 1982), pp. 208-229.
5. See Michael Gauvreau, *The Evangelical Century: Creed and College in English Canada from the Great Revival to the Great Depression* (unpublished manuscript, Kingston, 1987). It is my expectation that this important manuscript will be published in 1989 or 1990.
6. See H. H. Walsh, *The Christian Church in Canada* (Toronto, 1956), p. 149.
7. See A. Kewley, "Mass Evangelism in Upper Canada Before 1830," (Th.D. dissertation, Victoria University, Toronto, 1960).
8. See F. Asbury, *The Journal and Letters of Francis Asbury*, III (Nashville, 1958), pp. 341-345.
9. G. A. Phoebus, ed., *Beams of Light on Early Methodism on America* (New York, 1887), p. 142.
10. Quoted in Hatch, *The Democratization of American Christianity*, p. 72.
11. Ibid., p. 76.
12. See R. Isaac, *The Transformation of Virginia* (Chapel Hill, N.C., 1982), p. 316.
13. Ibid.
14. Ibid., p. 323.
15. Ibid., p. 324.
16. Ibid., p. 347.
17. Ibid., p. 357.
18. J. Carroll, *Case and His Contemporaries*, Vol. I (Toronto, 1867), pp. 114-118.
19. R. B. Nye, *The Unembarrassed Muse* (New York, 1970), pp. 4-5.
20. J. G. Ortega, *Man and Crisis* (New York, 1958), p. 120.
21. See R. Carwardine, *Trans-Atlantic Revivalism: Popular Evangelicalism in Britain and America 1790-1865* (Westport, Conn., 1978).
22. Quoted in P. Bush, "James Caughey, Phoebe and Walter Palmer and the Methodist Revival Experience in Canada West 1850-1858" (unpublished M.A. dissertation, Queen's University, 1985), p. 23.
23. John Carroll, *Case and His Contemporaries*, or, *the Canadian Itinerant's Memorial*, Vol. 3 (Toronto, 1871), pp. 491-492.
24. Carwardine, *Trans-Atlantic Revivalism*, p. 11.
25. See G. A. Rawlyk, "Kingston Baptists in the 19th Century" (unpublished paper, Queen's University, 1986).
26. *Christian Guardian*, Feb. 9, 1853.
27. W. H. Pearson, *Recollections...* (Toronto, 1914), pp. 322-323.
28. P. Bush, "The Reverend James Caughey and Wesleyan Methodist Revivalism in Canada West," *Ontario History*, Vol. LXXIX, No. 3 (Sept. 1987), pp. 247-248.
29. Bush, "James Caughey, Phoebe and Walter Palmer," pp. 93-94.

30. Ibid., p. 95.
31. United Church Archives, Minutes of the Sydenham Street Methodist Church.
32. This reference and all other references to the First Baptist Church, Kingston, are based upon the First Baptist Church Records, in the possession of Professor G. A. Rawlyk, Queen's University, and also to be found in the Canadian Baptist Archives, McMaster Divinity College.
33. *Montreal Register*, March 23, 1842.
34. First Baptist Church Records.
35. See D. Swainson, "Garden Island and the Calvin Company" (Kingston Marine Museum Pamphlet, n.d.), pp. 6-16.
36. Ibid., p. 6.
37. Bush, "James Caughey, Phoebe and Walter Palmer," p. 94.
38. Turner, *The Ritual Process*, pp. 94-140.

CHAPTER VI

1. A popular, largely uncritical biography of Sidey was written in 1976 by Gertrude A. Palmer. See her *The Combatant* (Middleton, N.S., 1976). Some of the material in this chapter is to be found in my "Fundamentalism, Modernism and the Maritime Baptists in the 1920s and 1930s," *Acadiensis* XIII (Fall 1987), pp. 3-33.
2. A statement about Sidey by the Reverend Perry Rockwood; quoted in Palmer, *The Combatant*, p. 195.
3. See J. J. Sidey, "The Widow's Mites" (unpublished autobiography, 1961); in the possession of G. A. Rawlyk, Kingston, Ontario.
4. Ibid.
5. Palmer, *The Combatant*, p. 25.
6. Ibid., p. 26.
7. Ibid.
8. "The Kingston Parsonage Case Records," A.U.A.
9. Sidey, "The Widow's Mites."
10. "The Kingston Parsonage Case Records," A.U.A.
11. *Sidey*, "The Widow's Mites."
12. Palmer, *The Combatant*, p. 32.
13. "The Kingston Parsonage Case Records," A.U.A.
14. Sidey, "The Widow's Mites."
15. Quoted in Palmer, *The Combatant*, p. 39.
16. Ibid.
17. Quoted in Palmer, *The Combatant*, p. 41.
18. N. Furniss, *The Fundamentalist Controversy 1918-1931* (New Haven, Conn., 1954), p. 36.
19. For information about the Soul Winner's Association, see Nova Scotia publication *The Challenge*, a microfilm copy of which is to be found in the P.A.N.S.
20. "Daily Programme of the Soul Winner's Festival, July 1–July 16, 1922," P.A.N.S.
21. See *The Challenge* for 1923.
22. Quoted in Palmer, *The Combatant*, p. 54.
23. Quoted in Palmer, *The Combatant*, p. 54.
24. See Turner, *The Ritual Process*, pp. 139-140.
25. Quoted in Palmer, *The Combatant*, p. 56.
26. Sidey, "The Widow's Mites."
27. Ibid.

28. J. Carpenter, "The Renewal of American Fundamentalism" (unpublished Ph.D. dissertation, Johns Hopkins University, 1984), p. 5.
29. E. R. Sandeen, *The Roots of Fundamentalism: British and American Millenarianism 1800-1930* (Chicago, 1970).
30. G. M. Marsden, *Fundamentalism and American Culture: The Shaping of Twentieth-Century Evangelicalism* (New York, 1980).
31. A. T. Doyle, *Front Benches and Back Rooms* (Toronto, 1976), pp. 85-97.
32. Palmer, *The Combatant*, p. 72.
33. Ibid.
34. Ibid., p. 74. See also the *Gospel Witness*, Aug. 20, 1925.
35. *Gospel Witness*, Aug. 20, 1925.
36. Palmer, *The Combatant*, p. 74.
37. *Maritime United Baptist Year Book 1927* (Truro, N.S., 1927), p. 14.
38. Ibid.
39. Quoted in Palmer, *The Combatant*, p. 160.
40. Quoted in Palmer, *The Combatant*, p. 196.
41. H. Harding to Thomas Bennett, April 21, 1792 in Rawlyk, *New Light Letters and Songs*, p. 166.

EPILOGUE

1. Quoted in Hatch, *The Democratization of American Christianity*, p. 77.
2. Quoted in G. Marsden, *Reforming Fundamentalism: Fuller Seminary and the New Evangelicalism* (Grand Rapids, 1987), p. 31.
3. See R. W. Fox and J. J. Jackson Lears, eds., *The Culture of Consumption*, (New York, 1983), p. xi.
4. Ibid., p. xi.
5. Ibid., pp. xi-xii.
6. T. Harpur, *For Christ's Sake* (Toronto, 1986), p. 53.
7. D. W. Frank, *Less Than Conquerors* (Grand Rapids, 1986), p. 222.
8. Quoted in Frank, *Less Than Conquerors*, p. 222.
9. Ibid., p. 223.
10. K. Marx and F. Engels, *The Communist Manifesto* (New York, 1964), p. 63.
11. Furniss, *The Fundamentalist Controversy 1918-1931*, p. 36.
12. R. W. Bibby and M. B. Brinkerhoff, "The Circulation of the Saints: A Study of People Who Join Conservative Churches," *Journal for the Scientific Study of Religion*, 1973, XII, pp. 273-283.
13. Quoted in Frank, *Less Than Conquerors*, p. 264.
14. Quoted in Frank, *Less Than Conquerors*, p. 264.
15. Ibid., p. 277.
16. Ibid.
17. Quoted in Frank, *Less Than Conquerors*, p. 277.

AFTERWORD

1. See the cogent summary of the Wallace thesis in W. G. McLoughlin, *Revivals, Awakenings and Reform: An Essay on Religion and Social Change in America 1607-1977* (Chicago, 1978), pp. 12-23.
2. Quoted in McLoughlin, *Revivals*, p. 15.
3. Ibid., p. 15.
4. Ibid., p. 16.
5. Ibid., p. 17.

6. Quoted in McLoughlin, *Revivals*, p. 17. See P. Worsley, *The Trumpet Shall Sound* (London, 1968).
7. See Bishop Charles Inglis to the Reverend J. Bailey, April 3, 1799, Public Archives of Nova Scotia, MG1, Vol. 93(a).
8. Ibid.
9. See the important article by L. I. Sweet in his edited volume *The Evangelical Tradition in America* (Macon, Ga., 1984), p. 37.
10. Turner, *The Ritual Process*, pp. 94-140.
11. See the very critical review by Gordon Stewart in the *Journal of the Canadian Church Historical Society*, 28 (1986), pp. 45-46.
12. Goodwin, p. 7.
13. Ibid., pp. 6-7.
14. See his *From Puritan to Yankee* (Cambridge, 1967).
15. G. A. Rawlyk, "Nova Scotia and the American Revolution," *New Edinburgh Review*, No. 35/6 (1976), pp. 107-108.
16. See G. A. Rawlyk and Gordon Stewart, "Nova Scotia's Sense of Mission," *Social History/Histoire Sociale*, II (1968), pp. 5-17.
17. See the French review/article, "Religion and Society in Late Eighteenth Century Nova Scotia," in *Acadiensis*, IV, No. 2 (Spring 1975), p. 107.
18. See some of the comments concerning the book on the back cover of the 1982 paperback edition.
19. Marsden, *Fundamentalism*, pp. 229-30. With author's acknowledgement of Joy L. Johnson, "The Theology of Middle-earth," (M.A. dissertation, Trinity Evangelical Divinity School, 1978).
20. Marsden, *Fundamentalism*, p. 230.

Index